Third-Grade Essentials

Carson-Dellosa Publishing LLC
Greensboro, North Carolina

Credits

Compiled by: Marie Shepherd

Content Editors: Nancy Rogers Bosse and Elizabeth Swenson

Copy Editor: Julie B. Killian

Layout and Cover Design: Lori Jackson

Cover Illustration: Ray Lambert

This book has been correlated to state, common core state, national, and Canadian provincial standards. Visit *www.carsondellosa.com* to search for and view its correlations to your standards.

Carson-Dellosa Publishing LLC
PO Box 35665
Greensboro, NC 27425 USA
www.carsondellosa.com

ISBN 978-1-60996-476-4
01-335111151

Table of Contents

● = Group Work   ★ = Extra Materials   ▲ = Cross-Curricular

Table of Contents

● = Group Work   ★ = Extra Materials   ▲ = Cross-Curricular

CD-104538 • © Carson-Dellosa

Table of Contents

● = Group Work   ★ = Extra Materials   ▲ = Cross-Curricular

Table of Contents

CD-104538 • © Carson-Dellosa

● = Group Work   ★ = Extra Materials   ▲ = Cross-Curricular

Table of Contents

● = Group Work   ★ = Extra Materials   ▲ = Cross-Curricular

CD-I04538 • © Carson-Dellosa

Introduction

Third-Grade Essentials offers activities for a full year of practice fun! Designed with the busy teacher in mind, this book is full of ready-to-go practice pages. The activities are both simple and engaging and will provide hours of learning fun.

Parents will love *Third-Grade Essentials* too! These fun and engaging activities are perfect for basic skills practice at home or on the go. The book covers an entire year of skills and provides practice tools that children will enjoy. *Third-Grade Essentials* includes the following skills:

Language Arts Skills:

- phonics
- synonyms and antonyms
- homophones
- reading comprehension
- sequence of events
- parts of speech

- compound words
- contractions
- story elements
- cause and effect
- writing and composition

Math Skills:

- number sense
- algebra
- skip counting
- fractions
- addition and subtraction
- probability
- multiplication and division

- geometry
- measurement
- time and money
- graphing
- problem solving
- place value

Each activity targets skills that are fundamental to third grade. Many activities also connect with science or social studies curriculums. *Third-Grade Essentials* follows national curriculum standards so that teachers can coordinate many of these easy-to-use practice activities with specific units of study.

Third-Grade Essentials is teacher tested and includes many helpful features:

- A comprehensive table of contents identifies activities by skill.

- Each activity's skill is identified in the upper right corner for quick reference.

- Icons in the table of contents make it easy to find activities with a cross-curricular connection.

- Every page includes two fun bonus activities to engage students further.

- Bonus activities that require extra materials or small groups are clearly marked by icons in the table of contents.

CD-104538 • © Carson-Dellosa

All About Town

This map shows the stops a bus makes on its route from North Station to South Station. Write the names of the stops in alphabetical order to figure out what route the bus traveled. Then, use a crayon to trace the bus route.

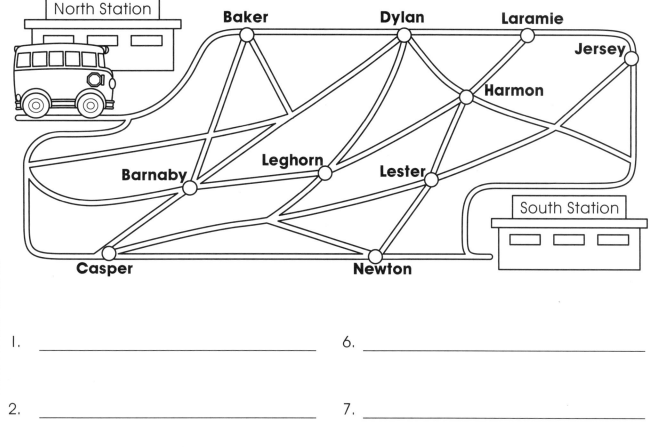

CD-104538 • © Carson-Dellosa

1. _____   6. _____

2. _____   7. _____

3. _____   8. _____

4. _____   9. _____

5. _____   10. _____

Try This!

A. On another sheet of paper, write a paragraph to describe the route the bus traveled. Be sure to use transition words, such as *first*, *then*, and *next*.

B. Look at a map of your state. On another sheet of paper, write the names of 20 cities in alphabetical order.

Dive Deep

Write the diving words in alphabetical order.

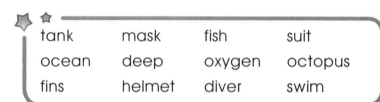

tank	mask	fish	suit
ocean	deep	oxygen	octopus
fins	helmet	diver	swim

1. _____   7. _____

2. _____   8. _____

3. _____   9. _____

4. _____   10. _____

5. _____   11. _____

6. _____   12. _____

 **Try This!**

A. Think of 10 things you might find at the bottom of the ocean. On another sheet of paper, list the words in alphabetical order.

B. Write a sentence with at least five words where each word in the sentence is in alphabetical order. For example: A diver dove down into the water.

CD-104538 • © Carson-Dellosa

System Overload

Write the video game titles in alphabetical order on the lines. Then, solve the riddle.

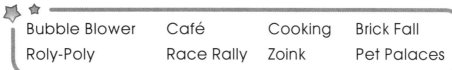

| Bubble Blower | Café | Cooking | Brick Fall |
| Roly-Poly | Race Rally | Zoink | Pet Palaces |

1. ___ ___ ___ ___ ☆ ___ ___ ___ ___ ___

2. ___ ___ ___ ___ ● ___ ___ ___ ___ ___ ___ ___

3. ___ ___ ■ ___ ___

4. ___ ___ ___ ___ * ___ ___ ___

5. ___ ___ ◆ ___ ___ ___ ___ ___ ___ ✓ ___

6. ___ ___ ▼ ___ ___ ___ ___ ___

7. ___ ___ ___ ___ ‐ ___ → ___ ___ ___

8. ___ ___ ○ ___ ___ ___

CD-104538 • © Carson-Dellosa

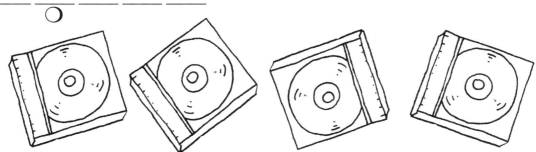

What starts with _P_, ends with _E_, and has a million letters in it?

___ ___ ___ ___ ___ ___ ___ ___ ___ ___ ___ ___ !
▼   →   ○   ✓   ◆   ○   ■   ■   *   ☆   ●

 **Try This!**

A. Write the first name of every student in your class in alphabetical order. Use the back of this paper.

B. Select 20 items from around the classroom. Ask a friend to time you as you place them in alphabetical order by name.

Clowning Around

Add a word part from the word bank to each blend to make a word that describes something a clown might do in his act.

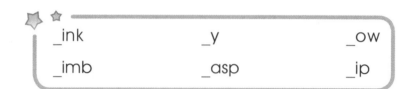

_ink   _y   _ow

_imb   _asp   _ip

bl   **fl**   **cl**

_____   _____   clown

_____   _____   _____

Try This!

A. On another sheet of paper, write a list of action words that start with *bl*, *cl*, or *fl*.

B. On another sheet of paper, write a story about these three clowns. Use the words from this page.

Name: _____

Twelve Swans Standing Still

Write the two letters that make up each word's beginning blend. Write *st*, *sw*, or *tw*.

1.

iche tesnnt

2.

Stamp

3.
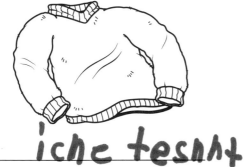
twins

4.

chan

5.

litFlash

6.

twenty

 **Try This!**

A. On another sheet paper, draw pictures of five other objects with names that start with *st*, *sw*, or *tw*. Have a friend figure out which blends the words begin with.

B. On another sheet paper, write five sentences that include as many words starting with *st*, *sw*, or *tw* as possible. For example: Twins stood on stools in matching sweaters.

Stay on the Path

Write *ow* or *ou* to correctly complete each word.

1. sc _____ t

2. m _____ ntain

3. tr _____ t

4. fl _____ er

5. sh _____ t

6. sh _____ er

7. t _____ er

8. c _____ nt

Try This!

A. On another sheet of paper, list five *ow* words and five *ou* words. Write a sentence using as many of the words as possible.

B. On another sheet of paper, write a story about a hike in the mountains. Use as many *ou* and *ow* words as possible.

Pizza Path

Find the path connecting each pair of rhyming words. Circle the *ow* in each word.

| prowl | power | bow | down | powder |

| scowl | brow | town | tower | chowder |

Try This!

A. Write five more pairs of rhyming *ow* words.

B. On another sheet of paper, draw a large pepperoni pizza. On each piece of pepperoni, write a different *ow* word.

Say Cheese!

Write *ch*, *sh*, or *th* to complete each word.

 __th__ umb

 __Sh__ irt

 __ch__ eese

 __Sh__ oe

 _____ orn

 __ch__ eck

 __ch__ in

 __Sh__ ell

 _____ ermos

★ **Try This!** ★

A. On another sheet of paper, list five other words for each of the beginning digraphs *ch*, *sh*, and *th*.

B. On another sheet of paper, write a story using as many *ch*, *sh*, and *th* words as possible.

Scavenger Hunt

Part of a scavenger hunt list was torn. Figure out what needs to be found by completing each word with the *ft*, *nt*, or *st* ending.

1. te _____

2. ne _____

3. ra _____

4. a _____

5. pla _____

6. fore _____

7. something so_____

8. footpri _____

CD-104538 • © Carson-Dellosa

Try This!

A. On another sheet of paper, write four more words with *ft*, *nt*, or *st* blends.

B. Using those words, write a story about a boy who has gone on a scavenger hunt.

Inch Along

Circle the word that names each picture.

couch   pouch

bush   brush

mouse   mouth

wreath   wrist

bath   bash

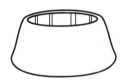

ditch   dish

beach   bench

fish   wish

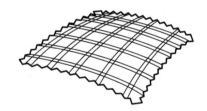

clock   cloth

 Try This!

A. Open a book and find six words that end with *ch*, *sh*, or *th*. Write the words on the back of this paper.

B. Write three silly sentences using at least four words with the same *ch*, *sh*, or *th* ending. Example: I will sit on a couch and eat a peach while I teach my brother to draw a finch.

Compound Connections

Cut out the cards below. Combine pairs of cards to form compound words. Glue the cards together on another sheet of paper. Then, draw a picture for each compound word.

CD-104538 • © Carson-Dellosa

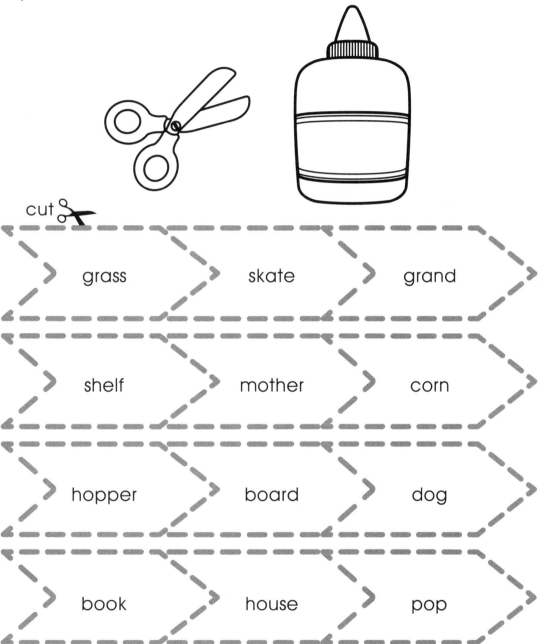

cut

grass	skate	grand
shelf	mother	corn
hopper	board	dog
book	house	pop

Try This!

A. On another sheet of paper, write a story using at least five of the above compound words.

B. Think of 10 new compound words. Write each word part on its own card. Then, play a memory game, matching each pair of words that forms a compound word.

Before and After

Write words from the word bank before and after each word to form compound words. Use each word only once.

Example: | every | body | guard |

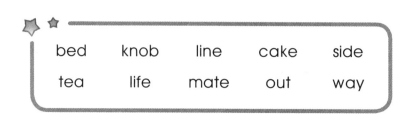

bed   knob   line   cake   side

tea   life   mate   out   way

1. [＿＿＿] door [＿＿＿]

2. [＿＿＿] cup [＿＿＿]

3. [＿＿＿] room [＿＿＿]

4. [＿＿＿] time [＿＿＿]

5. [＿＿＿] walk [＿＿＿]

 **Try This!**

A. On the back of this paper, use each compound word above in a sentence.

B. Find 20 other compound words in a dictionary. List them on another sheet of paper.

Syllable Hunt

Write words to match each clue. Use a dictionary if needed.

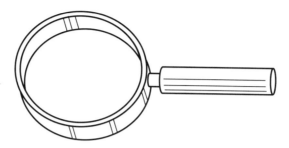

1. Three animal names with two syllables.

   _____   _____   _____

2. Two words with four syllables. Divide the words into syllables.

   _____   _____

3. Three parts of the body with one syllable.

   _____   _____   _____   _____

4. Three names with three syllables. Make sure to capitalize each name.

   _____   _____   _____

5. One word with five syllables. Divide the word into syllables.

   _____

6. One word with six syllables. Divide the word into syllables.

   _____

A. Ask a friend to play a syllable game. Roll a die. Think of a word that has the same number of syllables as the number on the die. Say the word aloud. Score one point for each syllable. Take turns. The first player to reach 20 points wins.

B. On the back of this paper, write a strategy for figuring out how many syllables a word has.

Planetary Patterns

Use the code to color the outer space word cards. Then, cut out the cards and arrange them to form a pattern. Glue the pattern on another sheet of paper.

1 syllable = blue   2 syllables = red
3 syllables = green   4 syllables = yellow

planet	orbit	sun	meteorite
Venus	Earth	Mars	Jupiter
Saturn	Uranus	Neptune	Mercury
moon	constellation	star	astronomer

cut

CD-104538 • © Carson-Dellosa

Try This!

A. Research the names of five stars or constellations. List the names on the back of this paper. Divide the names into syllables.

B. On another sheet of paper, draw our solar system and label the planets, moon, and stars. Use as many words from the cards as possible.

Jump Right In!

Draw lines to separate words with more than one syllable. Do not draw lines for words with only one syllable. Then, write the number of syllables.

1. jumping _____   6. bounce _____

2. hurdle _____   7. leap _____

3. outside _____   8. helmet _____

4. exercise _____   9. backyard _____

5. success _____   10. hopping _____

Write words that have one, two, and three syllables.

One Syllable	Two Syllables	Three Syllables
1. _____	1. _____	1. _____
2. _____	2. _____	2. _____
3. _____	3. _____	3. _____
4. _____	4. _____	4. _____
5. _____	5. _____	5. _____

A. On the back of this paper, list 20 words found in your classroom. Divide each word into syllables.

B. On another sheet of paper, list 10 words about your favorite outdoor activity. Divide each word into syllables.

Polly Want a Contraction?

Write the correct contraction from Polly's perch beside the words that make up the contraction.

isn't   I'm   you're   they've   we're

she's   don't   it's   haven't   we'll

1. I am _____

2. we are _____

3. they have _____

4. we will _____

5. she is _____

6. do not _____

7. is not _____

8. it is _____

9. you are _____

10. have not _____

A. On the back of this paper, use each contraction above in a sentence.

B. On another sheet of paper, write two contractions for each of the following words: *are, is, have, has, will, would,* and *not.*

Star-Studded Work

Write the two words that make up each contraction.

1. aren't
_____

4. he's
_____

7. they're
_____

2. she'll
_____

5. you'll
_____

8. I'm
_____

3. you're
_____

6. we're
_____

9. can't
_____

A. On the back of this paper, use each contraction above in a sentence.

B. On another sheet of paper, list as many contractions as you can think of.

Cooking Up Prefixes

Read each clue. Use the prefix *un-*, *dis-*, or *re-* to write a word that means the same. Then, find and circle your answers in the puzzle.

d	i	s	r	e	u	n	d	r	e	s	u
r	e	b	u	i	l	d	i	s	l	a	k
a	d	r	n	n	o	i	n	r	e	d	o
r	l	u	n	u	n	s	a	f	e	r	u
s	a	g	r	e	e	o	b	r	f	o	n
r	e	f	i	l	l	b	r	e	f	i	f
o	u	t	r	y	s	e	b	u	l	o	r
u	n	h	a	p	p	y	u	n	d	e	i
s	t	e	d	r	e	w	r	i	t	e	e
u	r	t	s	o	r	e	w	o	s	n	n
u	n	d	i	s	a	p	p	e	a	r	d
b	r	d	r	w	p	i	w	n	s	i	l
p	e	n	a	u	n	f	o	l	d	e	y
r	e	b	u	n	t	l	d	i	m	b	e

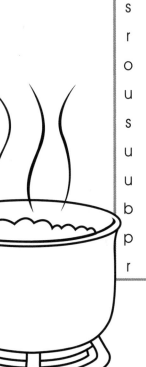

CD-104538 • © Carson-Dellosa

1. not happy _____

2. not obey _____

3. not safe _____

4. fill again _____

5. not appear_____

6. write again _____

7. not fold_____

8. do again _____

9. not friendly _____

10. build again _____

A. Use a highlighter to highlight each prefix in the puzzle. Then, use a different color of highlighter to highlight each base word.

B. Write a story using as least 10 words with the prefixes *un-*, *dis-*, or *re-*.

Buzzing Around

Cut out the pieces of honeycomb at the bottom of the page. Pair pieces of honeycomb to form new words to match the clues. Glue each pair on the honeycomb.

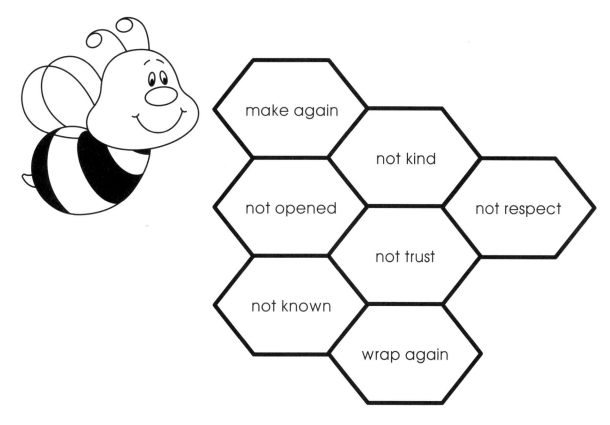

make again

not kind

not opened

not respect

not trust

not known

wrap again

Try This!

A. On another sheet of paper, use each new word on the honeycomb in a sentence.

B. On another sheet of paper, write the base word of each word above. Use a different prefix with each word. Then, write the new word and its definition.

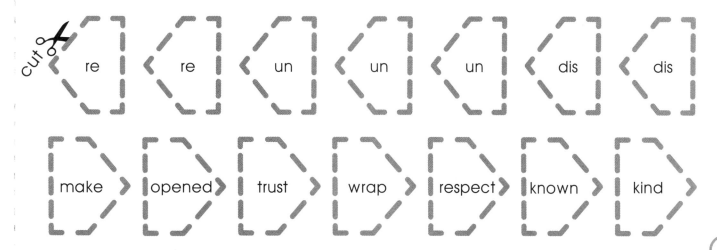

Cut

re   re   un   un   un   dis   dis

make   opened   trust   wrap   respect   known   kind

Lizard Tails

Cut out the cards. Glue the suffix cards to the top of another sheet of paper.
Then, glue each card under the correct suffix. Write the new word.

A. On the back of this paper, use each word formed below in a sentence about lizards.

B. On another sheet of paper, write a paragraph about lizards. Use as many words from the cards as possible.

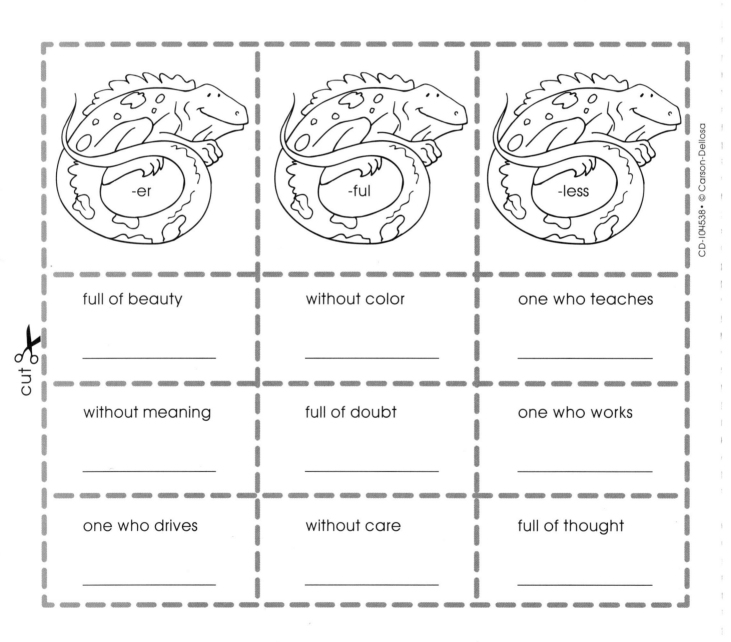

-er	-ful	-less
full of beauty	without color	one who teaches
_____	_____	_____
without meaning	full of doubt	one who works
_____	_____	_____
one who drives	without care	full of thought
_____	_____	_____

cut ✂

Name: _____

The End

Use the suffixes *-en*, *-ment*, and *-able* to form words to complete the puzzle.

Across

1. something that governs
3. to make harder
4. able to be washed
5. something that is developed
9. something that is shipped

Down

2. able to be read
6. to make lighter
7. able to be enjoyed
8. to make tighter

A. On the back of this paper, use some of the answers from the puzzle to write a riddle to tell your friends.

B. On another sheet of paper, write 12 other words that have the *-able*, *-en*, or *-ment* suffix. Then, write the meaning of each word.

On the Road Again

Rewrite each word, adding -er and -est. The first one has been done for you.

1. small   _____smaller_____   _____smallest_____

2. strange   _____   _____

3. bright   _____   _____

4. pretty   _____   _____

5. dirty   _____   _____

Circle the word that best completes each sentence.

6. My family drove to see the _____ ball of string in the world.

         big   bigger   biggest

7. Our RV drives _____ than your RV.

         fast   faster   fastest

8. Of the three of us, I had the _____ luggage.

         heavy   heavier   heaviest

9. This was the _____ trip ever!

         cool   cooler   coolest

Try This!

A. On the back of this paper, use each word in a sentence: *smart*, *smarter*, and *smartest*.

B. On another sheet of paper, make a poster to explain the rule of when to use *-er* and when to use *-est*.

Synonym Clues

Write a word from the word bank that has nearly the same meaning as each clue. Use a thesaurus to help you.

academy	bandana	crate
fancy	lurch	nation
rhythm	rickety	section

Across

2. area

5. beat

8. scarf

9. unstable

Down

1. school

3. wobble

4. country

6. box

7. elaborate

A. Find at least one more synonym for each clue. Write your answers on the back of this paper. Use a thesaurus to help you.

B. Find an ad in a newspaper or a magazine. On another sheet of paper, rewrite the ad using synonyms.

Opposites Attract

Cut out the cards. On another sheet of paper, glue each pair of antonyms together.

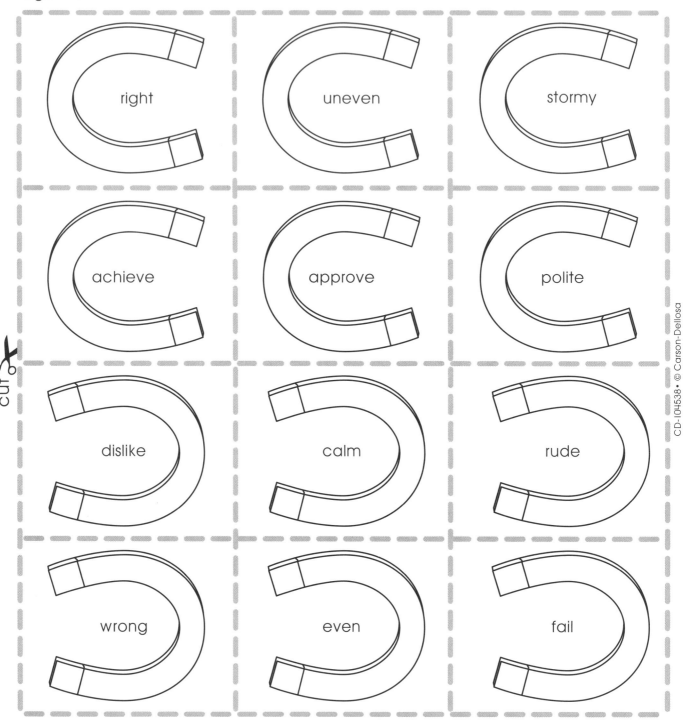

right

uneven

stormy

achieve

approve

polite

dislike

calm

rude

wrong

even

fail

cut

Try This!

A. On the back of this paper, write five more opposite pairs.

B. On another sheet of paper, write an opposites poem using some of the antonyms on this page.

Name: _____

Fishing for Opposites

Find the pairs of antonyms. Write the words on the lines.

 sharp

 small

 buy

 big

 good

 weak

 raw

 lock

 unlock

 present

 cooked

 strong

 bad

 absent

 dull

 sell

_____ and _____   _____ and _____

_____ and _____   _____ and _____

_____ and _____   _____ and _____

_____ and _____   _____ and _____

⭐ **Try This!** ⭐

A. On the back of this paper, explain why you think it is important to know synonyms and antonyms of words.

B. On another sheet of paper, write the word *dull* in large letters. Then, cross out the word and draw pictures to illustrate the antonyms of *dull*.

Same and Different

Complete the chart by writing a synonym for each word in the first column and an antonym for each word in the second column.

Synonyms		Antonyms
	big	
	happy	
	short	
	fast	
	easy	
	quiet	
	warm	
	bright	

CD-104538 • © Carson-Dellosa

Try This!

A. On the back of this paper, write another synonym and antonym for each word above.

B. List the letters of the alphabet on another sheet of paper. Write a word that begins with each letter. Then, write an antonym for the word. For example: **a**fter/before, **b**oy/ girl, **c**lose/open, etc.

Four in a Row

Read each pair of words. If the words are synonyms, circle them. If the words are antonyms, cross them out.

delicious/tasty	front/back	shout/yell	first/last
dirty/filthy	clean/tidy	hot/cold	sloppy/neat
bland/tasteless	huge/small	large/gigantic	afraid/scared
hungry/satisfied	laugh/giggle	smart/intelligent	thin/slim

Try This!

A. Change each antonym pair into a synonym pair by changing one of the words. Then, change each synonym pair into an antonym pair by changing one of the words.

B. Make a book of opposites to share with a younger child.

Wacky Word Pairs

Answer each question with a pair of words that sound the same but have different meanings. The first one has been done for you.

1. What do you call a bald grizzly? _____ a bare bear _____

2. What do you call a mare with a sore throat? _____

3. What do you call a sweet doe? _____

4. What do you call an evening with a man in shining armor? _____

5. What do you call a frail seven days? _____

6. What do you call a reasonable cost of a bus ride? _____

7. What do you call a great trick with things you walk on? _____

8. What does a small insect call his uncle's wife? _____

CD-104538 • © Carson-Dellosa

Try This! _____

A. On the back of this paper, write each pair of homophones in a sentence.

B. On another sheet of paper, write three more homophones.

Can You Hear Me?

Unscramble the letters to write each pair of homophones.

_____ (dad)   _____ (da)

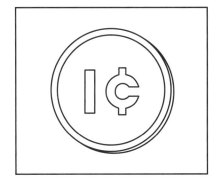

_____ (geith)   _____ (eat)

_____ (etcsn)   _____ (tnce)

 **Try This!**

A. On the back of this paper, write a definition for each word you wrote above.

B. On another sheet of paper, use each word from above in a sentence.

Could It Happen?

Each sentence has a pair of homographs. Read the sentence and circle the correct answer.

1. Could a man with a bow bow?   yes   no

2. Could you present your friend with a present?   yes   no

3. Can a tear tear?   yes   no

4. Will a door close if you get too close?   yes   no

5. Would a doctor have wound a bandage around that wound?   yes   no

6. Could the wind wind your watch?   yes   no

7. Could lead lead the parade?   yes   no

8. Do live animals live in the wild?   yes   no

⭐ **Try This!** ⭐

A. Underline the homographs above. Then, write the meaning of each homograph on the back of this paper.

B. On another sheet of paper, write five sentences using a homograph pair in each sentence.

In Nature

Read each sentence. Then, circle the letter for the correct definition of the underlined word as it is used in the sentence.

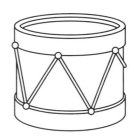

blow	a. hit; b. breathe out hard	**box**	a. fight; b. container
buck	a. dollar (slang); b. male deer	**drum**	a. beat or pound; b. musical instrument
peer	a. one of the same age; b. look at closely	**sharp**	a. pointed; b. alert or observant

1. <u>Bucks</u> have large, strong antlers.   a   b

2. The buck's <u>sharp</u> eyes look out for danger.   a   b

3. When in danger, a buck will <u>drum</u> the ground.   a   b

4. A buck will stand on its hind legs to <u>box</u>.   a   b

5. A buck can deliver a hard <u>blow</u> with his antlers.   a   b

6. The young deer will <u>peer</u> over the tall grass.   a   b

A. On another sheet of paper, draw pictures to show some of the ways a buck will defend himself.

B. Create a multiple-meaning wordbook. Use a dictionary if needed.

Bookworm Part 1

Use a highlighter to highlight each entry word and its part of speech. Then, use this dictionary page to answer the questions on page 43.

absorption–organic

absorption (*n*) 1. the process of being absorbed 2. entire mind taken over by something

clay (*n*) an earthy material that is made up of minerals and is often used to make brick and pottery

compost (*n*) a mixture used for fertilizing land (*v*) to convert to compost

decompose (*v*) 1. to break down into simpler compounds 2. rot

erosion (*n*) the process of eroding

gravel (*n*) 1. sand 2. loose pieces of rock

humidity (*n*) wetness in the air

inorganic (*adj*) 1. made up of something other than plants or animals 2. artificial

microbe (*n*) germ

mineral (*n*) 1. ore 2. something that is neither animal nor vegetable

organic (*adj*) 1. produced without using chemicals 2. natural

A. Look up the above words in a dictionary. On the back of this paper, write the guide words for the page each word is on.

B. Look up 10 more words in the dictionary. Write the words and their definitions on another sheet of paper.

Bookworm Part 2

Answer the questions using the dictionary on page 42.

1. What is the quickest way to find out if the word *topsoil* will appear on this

   dictionary page? _____

2. What do the abbreviations *n, v,* and *adj* stand for?

   _____

3. How many definitions are given for the word *decompose*? _____

4. Write a sentence with the word *organic*.

   _____

5. Which word can be used as a noun or a verb? _____

6. What type of dictionary is this? How do you know?

   _____

7. Write two more words that could be included on this dictionary page.

   _____

8. Write two words that could not be included on this dictionary page.

   _____

Try This!

A. Use a real dictionary page to write questions for a friend to answer on the back of this paper.

B. On another sheet of paper, compare and contrast a dictionary and a glossary.

Guide Me

Look at the guide words at the top of each word list. Circle each word in the list that could be an entry word on a page with those guide words.

1. lead–lease	2. gift–globe	3. rude–rumor
lean	giant	royal
leap	give	ruler
left	glove	ruin
leaf	glass	ruby

4. puppet–python	5. acrobat–action	6. silly–single
pyramid	act	silver
pudding	acronym	sibling
puzzle	active	similar
pupil	acquaint	simile

A. Look up the entry words above in a dictionary. On the back of this paper, write the guide words for the page each word is on.

B. On another sheet of paper, write a paragraph to explain how and why guide words are used.

Making a Compass

Read the passage. Then, follow the directions.

How to Make a Compass

    Have you ever used a compass to find your way? A compass is a magnet that can identify geographic direction. It is easy to make your own compass, and it is a lot of fun too! First, you will need to make a sewing needle magnetic. To do this, rub the needle away from you across a magnet several times. Be sure to rub the needle in the same direction each time. Once the needle is magnetic, tape it to a small piece of plastic. Then, float the needle in a dish of water. Wait for your floating needle to stop spinning. In what direction is it pointing? What happens to the needle?

1. Underline all declarative sentences in red.

2. Underline all exclamatory sentences in orange.

3. Underline all imperative sentences in green.

4. Underline all interrogative sentences in blue.

  A. Use the same steps above to find different types of sentences in a newspaper comic strip.

  B. On another sheet of paper, write a story about someone who used a compass. Use all four types of sentences in your story.

Plants!

Cut out the flowerpots and glue them to the bottom of another sheet of paper. Add the correct punctuation to each sentence. Then, cut out and glue each sentence card above the correct flowerpot.

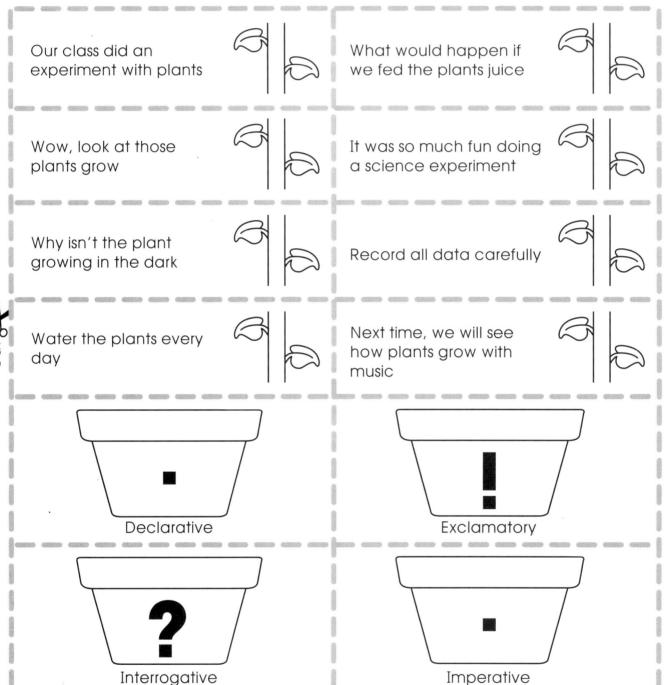

Our class did an experiment with plants

What would happen if we fed the plants juice

Wow, look at those plants grow

It was so much fun doing a science experiment

Why isn't the plant growing in the dark

Record all data carefully

Water the plants every day

Next time, we will see how plants grow with music

Declarative

Exclamatory

Interrogative

Imperative

CD-104538 • © Carson-Dellosa

Try This!

A. Add two more sentences to each flowerpot.

B. Search a newspaper and highlight an example of each type of sentence.

Name: _____

To the Moon!

Combine each pair of sentences using *and*, *or*, *but*, or *so*. Write each compound sentence on the line.

CD-104538 • © Carson-Dellosa

1. NASA built a spacecraft called *Apollo 11*. They launched it on July 16, 1969.

   _____

2. Four days later, *Apollo 11* reached the moon. On July 20, Neil Armstrong and Buzz Aldrin walked on the moon.

   _____

3. The astronauts took many pictures of the moon. They also collected 47 pounds of moon rocks.

   _____

4. You can read about their moonwalk online. You can read about it in history books.

   _____

A. On the back of this paper, write sentences using *and*, *or*, *but*, and *so*.

B. On another sheet of paper, write about what you think a trip to the moon would be like. Include at least three compound sentences.

Subject Sleuth

Write the correct verb to complete each sentence.

1. In the summer, I _____ as a detective. (work, works)

2. I _____ neighborhood mysteries. (solve, solves)

3. When my friends _____ things, I help my friends find them. (lose, loses)

4. Jamie _____ things often. (lose, loses)

5. My friend Julio _____ me secret messages. (write, writes)

6. I _____ my decoder to figure them out. (use, uses)

7. I _____ my detective kit in a secret place. (keep, keeps)

8. Only my mom and dad _____ where it is. (know, knows)

A. On the back of this paper, write a rule for choosing the correct verb.

B. On another sheet of paper, write an advertisement for a summer job you would like to have.

CD-104538 • © Carson-Dellosa

Mix and Match

Mix and match the subjects and the verbs to write six sentences. Be sure that your subjects and verbs agree.

Subjects	Verbs
Mom and Dad	talks
My sister	pick
I	explains
The boys	share
Tasha	tells
Mrs. Ortiz	earn

1. I _____

2. _____

3. _____

4. _____

5. _____

6. _____

Try This!

A. On the back of this paper, mix and match the subjects and the verbs in different ways to write six more sentences.

B. On another sheet of paper, write a story using the subjects and the verbs from above.

Star Code

Use the code to color the verbs.

present tense = yellow

past tense = orange

future tense = blue

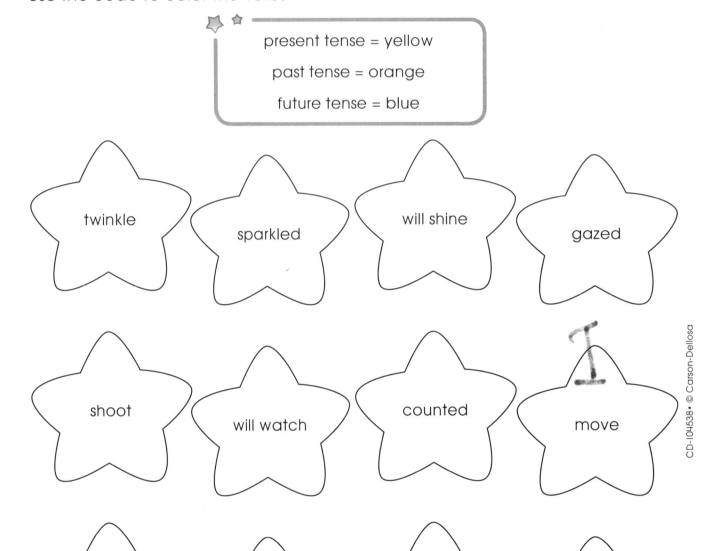

twinkle

sparkled

will shine

gazed

shoot

will watch

counted

move

looked

will fade

rise

will name

 **Try This!**

A. Cut out the completed stars and glue them to another sheet of paper to form a constellation of your choice.

B. On another sheet of paper, write about a time that you watched stars in the sky. Be sure to watch the tenses of your verbs.

Past and Future

Write the past tense and the future tense of each word.

 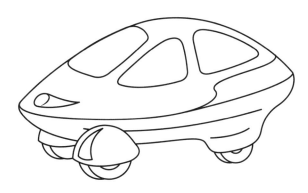

		Past Tense	Future Tense
1.	become	_____	_____
2.	ride	_____	_____
3.	come	_____	_____
4.	draw	_____	_____
5.	give	_____	_____
6.	drive	_____	_____
7.	take	_____	_____
8.	win	_____	_____

Try This!

A. On the back of this paper, use some of the verbs above to write a commercial for a brand-new model of car.

B. On another sheet of paper, compare cars of the past to cars of the future.

51

Growing Great Pronouns Part 1

Complete each cornstalk with nouns that could be replaced with the pronoun shown on the ear of corn.

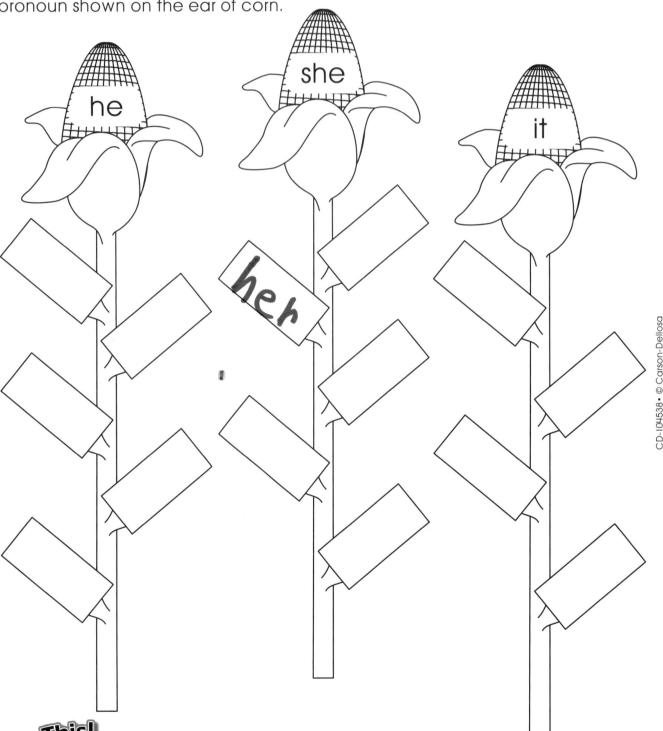

Try This!

A. On the back of this paper, list each person in your family. Then, write a pronoun for each person.

B. Find a paragraph in a book. Replace each common and proper noun with the correct pronoun.

Growing Great Pronouns Part 2

Complete each cornstalk with nouns that could be replaced with the pronoun shown on the ear of corn.

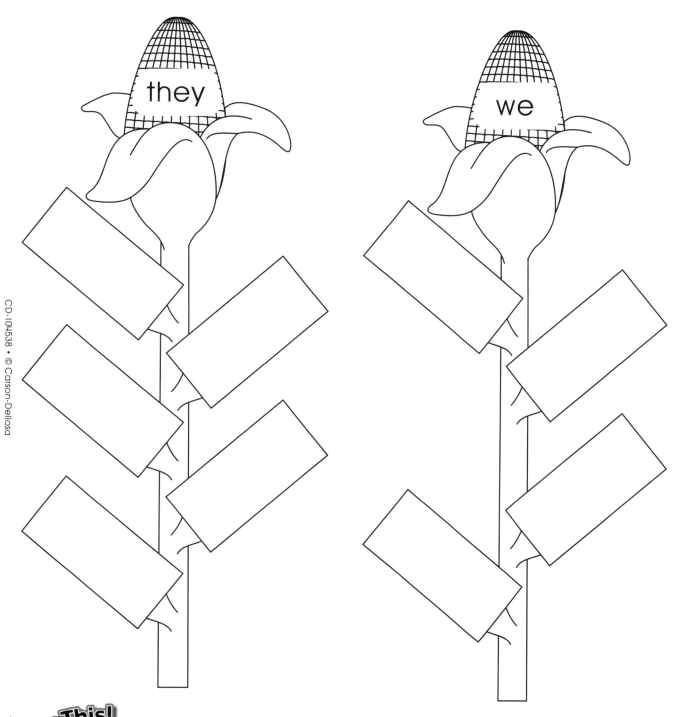

★ Try This! ★

A. On another sheet of paper, write a story with a cornfield as the setting. Use at least 10 pronouns in your story.

B. Cover at least 10 nouns in a book with sticky notes. Then, write a pronoun on each note to replace each noun.

Camping Out

Write a pronoun to replace each underlined word or words.

1. Last summer, <u>Uncle Nick</u> took me camping. _____

2. <u>My mom</u> helped me pack. _____

3. <u>Uncle Nick and I</u> set up camp. _____

4. <u>The rangers</u> at the campground welcomed us. _____

5. We told <u>the rangers</u> that we would stay two nights. _____

6. I helped <u>my uncle</u> build a campfire. _____

7. <u>Our campfire</u> kept us warm. _____

8. I told <u>my mom</u> about our trip when I got home. _____

A. On the back of this paper, write about an adventure you had with a family member. Use at least five pronouns.

B. List all of the above pronouns. Organize the list into subject pronouns and object pronouns.

CD-104538 • © Carson-Dellosa

Name: _____

Once Upon a Time

Write three adjectives to describe each of the fairy-tale characters.

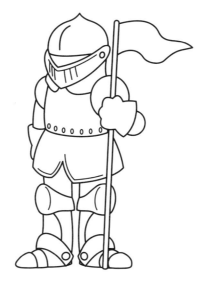

knight

_____

_____

_____

princess

_____

_____

_____

queen

_____

_____

_____

king

_____

_____

_____

giant

_____

_____

_____

prince

_____

_____

_____

A. On another sheet of paper, write a fairy tale using some of the words above.

B. Divide the back of this paper into three sections. Label the sections *Which One?*, *How Many?*, and *What Kind?* Then, list five adjectives that fit in each section.

Be More Specific

Complete the chart by writing specific adjectives to describe each noun.

	Which One?	How Many?	What Kind?
rules			
laws			
constitution			
citizen			
senator			
state			
judge			

CD-104538 • © Carson-Dellosa

A. On the back of this paper, write a sentence for each noun. Include some of the adjectives from above.

B. On another sheet of paper, write a paragraph about the U.S. Constitution. Include some of the adjectives from above.

One Box, Two Boxes

Write the plural form of each noun.

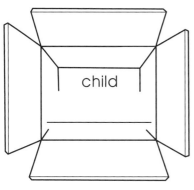

child

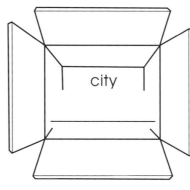

city

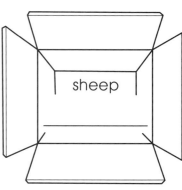

sheep

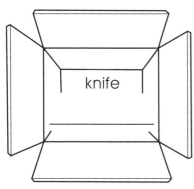

knife

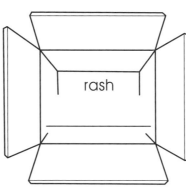

rash

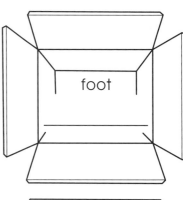

foot

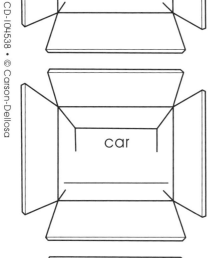

car

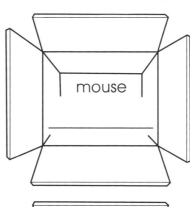

mouse

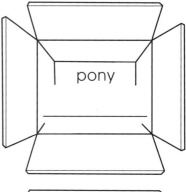

pony

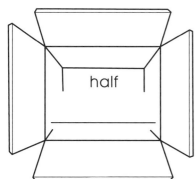

half

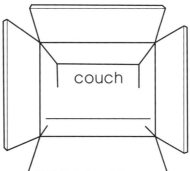

couch

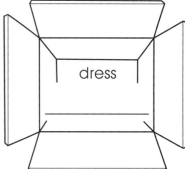

dress

CD-104538 • © Carson-Dellosa

 **Try This!**

A. On the back of this paper, use each plural noun in a sentence.

B. On another sheet of paper, write the rules for making plural nouns.

It's Raining Apostrophes!

Use a different possessive noun to complete each sentence.

1. The three _____ paws were wet.

2. The _____ room was messy.

3. The _____ pencil was broken.

4. Both _____ grades were good.

5. That is _____ house across the street.

6. Some _____ uniforms were the wrong color.

7. We saw two _____ tracks along the path.

8. The _____ mailboxes were painted red.

CD-104538 • © Carson-Dellosa

A. On the back of this paper, explain the difference between *dog's* and *dogs'*.

B. On another sheet of paper, write the rules for using apostrophes to show possession. Write a sentence as an example of each rule.

A Night on the Town

Write a proper noun for each common noun.

1. building _____

2. street _____

3. store _____

4. school _____

5. city _____

6. state _____

7. book _____

8. name _____

9. song _____

10. country _____

 **Try This!**

A. On the back of this paper, write a journal entry that explains the difference between a common noun and a proper noun. List examples of each.

B. In a newspaper article, circle all of the common nouns and underline all of the proper nouns.

Name: _____

Capitalization

Correct Capitals

Write *C* if the sentence uses capitals correctly. Write *X* if the sentence does not use capitals correctly. Rewrite each sentence with an *X* correctly.

_____ 1. "after lunch," said Reba, "let's go shopping."

_____ 2. Taron goes to hudson elementary school in forest park.

_____ 3. Have you visited Disneyland in California?

_____ 4. We saw the movie "sub sandwich sleuths" yesterday.

_____ 5. The letter to Ross ended, "Love, Aunt Rose."

_____ 6. the hansens live in los angeles, california.

_____

_____

_____

_____

_____

_____

_____

_____

_____

_____

⭐ **Try This!** ⭐

A. On another sheet of paper, make a poster listing the rules for capitalization.

B. Write a letter to your principal about an issue that is important to you. Be sure to use correct capitalization.

CD-104538 • © Carson-Dellosa

60

Name: _____

Name: _____

Capitalization

Happy Birthday to Me!

Complete the paragraph with information about your birthday. Cross out each letter that should be capitalized. Be sure to capitalize the words that you add if needed.

My Birthday

i love my birthday! my birthday is on ~~October~~ August _____.

i will be ___8 9___ years old on my next birthday. i was born on

___11th wen myB___ in ___weh my mom___ my family celebrates

my birthday with _____.

I like to eat _____

on my birthday. On one of my birthdays, we went to _____.

I had a great time!

 **Try This!** _____

    A. Write a final draft of the paragraph on another sheet of paper. Check your capitalization.

    B. On another sheet of paper, write about your best birthday. Provide a lot of details. Check your capitalization.

CD-104538 • © Carson-Dellosa

61

Honest Abe

Read each sentence. Place commas where they are needed.

1. Young Abraham was a happy calm and intelligent child.

2. His parents paid his teacher with firewood venison and potatoes.

3. Abe liked to tell jokes stories and tall tales.

4. Abe loved to read write and talk with people.

5. Abe worked as a storekeeper a surveyor a boatman and a postmaster.

6. He and his wife enjoyed music dancing and the theater.

7. Their four sons were named Robert Edward Willie and Tad.

8. President Lincoln helped free the slaves unite the North and South and keep the country united.

Try This!

A. On another sheet of paper, write about what you like to do. Include commas where they are needed.

B. Research another president of the United States. On another sheet of paper, write sentences that tell about him. Make sure each sentence lists items in a series.

A Few of My Favorite Things

Provide at least three answers to each question in one complete sentence. Remember to use commas where they are needed.

1. What are some of your favorite foods?

_____

2. Who are some of your favorite friends?

_____

3. What are some of your favorite games?

_____

4. What are some of your favorite books?

_____

5. Where are some of your favorite places to go?

_____

6. What are some of your favorite toys?

_____

 _____

A. Compare your sentences with those of a friend. On the back of this paper, write about things that you both like.

B. On another sheet of paper, write an essay about one of your favorites. Use one of the answers above as your topic sentence.

Create a Country

Add the missing punctuation to each sentence.

1. Pilar created her own country

2. She created her country on October 29 2011

3. What would her country be like

4. What would be the law of the land

5. She wanted all citizens to be equal

6. Men women and children would have the same rights

7. All races religions and cultures would be respected

8. Everyone would live in peace

CD-104538 • © Carson-Dellosa

 **Try This!**

A. On the back of this paper, describe a country that you would create. What would be the most important laws?

B. On another sheet of paper, design a flag for your country. Explain what each symbol and color stands for.

A Letter Home

Use proofreaders' marks to show the mistakes in Nellie's letter home. The letter includes 26 mistakes.

Proofreaders' Marks
≡   capital letter
lc   lowercase letter
∧   insert

january 20 2011

dearest mother

    I arrived in america safely. it is a very beautiful Country with lovely mountains trees and blue skies. I even saw a Deer in the woods.

    Yesterday I helped aunt sarah plant a garden we planted corn beans and carrots I can't wait to taste the vegetables.

    Tell father matthew and jonathan that i send my love. I miss you greatly and will write again soon.

love

Nellie

A. On another sheet of paper, rewrite the letter, correcting all of the mistakes.

B. Write a letter to a family member. Proofread your letter for capitalization and punctuation.

Snack Time!

Cut out the names of the snacks below. Glue each name under the correct snack.

1.
Just thaw and serve!
What a treat!

2.
**Fun to blow!
No sugar!**

3.
**Just add water,
mix, and heat!**

4.
*Fruity delicious!
Goes anywhere!*

5.
**Contains milk
and chocolate.
Nothing artificial added.**

6.
**Made with natural oats!
Goes anywhere!**

CD-104538 • © Carson-Dellosa

cut ✂

| Juicy Frozen Fruit | All-Natural Ice Cream | Sugar-Free Bubble Gum |
| Instant Oatmeal | Fruit Bar | Granola Bar |

 **Try This!**

A. On another sheet of paper, draw a picture of your favorite snack. Then, write a paragraph that describes it.

B. On another sheet of paper, write an advertisement for one of the packages shown. Be sure to use the main idea and supporting details from the package. Illustrate your advertisement.

My Name Is Amber

Read each paragraph. Underline the topic sentence twice. Underline the detail sentences once.

1. Amber Walsh hated her name. Without even trying, she could think of 20 better names. In fact, when her family moved to Lakeville, she thought about telling everyone that her name was Madison. She decided it was not a good idea. She might not turn around when someone said, "Madison."

2. One day, Amber read about amber in her science book. She learned that amber is a type of fossil made from tree sap. Some trees with layers of sap on their trunks aged and died. When they fell, they were covered with dirt or water. The trees were buried for millions of years.

 Try This!

A. On the back of this paper, explain the difference between the topic sentence and the detail sentences.

B. On another sheet of paper, write about your name. Be sure to include a topic sentence followed by at least three detail sentences.

Cross It Out

Read each paragraph. Underline the topic sentence twice. Underline the detail sentences once. Cross out the detail sentence that does not belong.

1. Yesterday my class visited the zoo. We were amazed at all of the animals that lived there. Animals from all over the world were in their natural habitats. My natural habitat is a house. My favorite animal was the elephant.

2. We played a game called Silent Ball. To play this game, everyone must stand in a circle and be very quiet. A sponge ball is then passed from person to person. The ball may be passed to a person next to you or to a person across the room. Miranda does not like the game, so she chose not to play. If a player misses the ball or makes a sound, he must sit down. The last person standing is the winner.

3. Jose has an unusual pet. It is an iguana named Spike. Spike lives in a glass house made from an old fish aquarium. He eats a special diet of fruit and green plants. Spike has a greenish-gray color and blends into his environment. My friend Mario has an unusual pet too. Jose's unusual pet is fun to observe.

Try This!

A. On the back of this paper, write a paragraph about something that has happened at school. Underline the topic sentence once. Underline the detail sentences twice.

B. On another sheet of paper, write how to play your favorite game. Be sure to include a topic sentence and at least three detail sentences.

How Seeds Spread

Cut out the topic sentences and glue them on another sheet of paper. Then, cut out the detail sentences and glue them under the correct topic sentence. Glue the labels to identify the topic sentences and the detail sentences.

Topic Sentences

Detail Sentences

Some seeds with spikes attach to animals' fur.	Dandelion seeds have parachutes.
Some sticky seeds attach to the feet of some animals.	Maple seeds have wings.
Animals eat seeds and move them to other locations through their waste.	The wind picks up some seeds and carries them.
The wind spreads seeds.	Animals spread seeds.

Try This!

A. On the back of this paper, rewrite each topic sentence and its supporting details in a paragraph.

B. For each detail sentence, write a paragraph using the sentence as a topic sentence.

Hop! Hop! Hop!

Read each paragraph. Underline the topic sentence twice. Underline the detail sentences once.

1. Rabbits like to live together in a group. They dig their burrows like underground apartments where they will always have a lot of neighbors. They help each other take care of their young. When the weather turns cold, they snuggle up together to keep each other warm.

2. The mother and father rabbit scratch a hole in the sandy wall of the burrow with their front feet. Then, they use their back feet to push the loose ground back into the tunnel. The mother rabbit smooths the walls and then pulls out pieces of her fur to line the floor. Both mother and father rabbit work hard to prepare a nursery for the babies that will soon be born.

Try This!

A. On the back of this paper, write a paragraph about your home that includes a topic sentence and three detail sentences.

B. Cut out a picture from a magazine and glue it to the top of another sheet of paper. Under the picture, write a topic sentence and three detail sentences about the picture.

The History of Money

Cut out the sentences. Glue them in the correct order on another sheet of paper.

Then, Alexis and Emma went to the local library.

Alexis and Emma decided to research the history of money.

After the report was written, Alexis and Emma made a display.

Alexis read the book and then told Emma all about it.

Finally, the girls presented their report to the class.

Alexis and Emma's teacher gave them a research project.

Emma wrote the information in a report.

First, they looked online for important information.

There they checked out a book called *The History of Money*.

 ✂ cut

Try This!

A. On another sheet of paper, write steps to explain how to buy a toy at a toy store.

B. Draw a cartoon about saving money. Your cartoon should illustrate each step in the correct order, such as earning money and putting money in a bank.

Pancake Breakfast

Read the recipe. Number the steps in the correct order.

Pancakes

Ingredients:

$\frac{3}{4}$ cup flour

1 tablespoon sugar

1 tablespoon baking powder

$\frac{1}{4}$ teaspoon salt

1 tablespoon melted butter

1 egg

$\frac{3}{4}$ cup milk

Steps:

_____ Cook the pancakes until they are lightly browned on both sides.

_____ In a small bowl, mix together melted butter, egg, and milk.

_____ Have an adult help you spoon $\frac{1}{4}$ cup of the pancake batter onto a heated skillet.

_____ In a large bowl, mix together flour, sugar, baking powder, and salt. Set aside.

_____ When bubbles start to appear in the pancake, flip it over with a spatula.

_____ Serve the pancakes with your favorite pancake topping and enjoy.

_____ Add the egg mixture to the flour mixture. Stir until it is well blended.

 **Try This!**

A. On the back of this paper, write about what might happen if the steps are not in the correct order.

B. On another sheet of paper, write a recipe for one of your favorite treats. Be sure to put the steps in the correct order.

Brush! Brush! Brush!

Cut out the sentences. Glue them in the correct order on another sheet of paper.

 Brush your top and bottom teeth.

 Rinse off your toothbrush until it is clean.

 Wet the toothbrush with water.

 Wipe your mouth.

 Take out your toothbrush and toothpaste.

 Brush your tongue.

 Squeeze the toothpaste onto your toothbrush.

 Spit out the toothpaste and rinse your mouth.

 Put away your toothbrush and toothpaste.

cut ✂

Try This!

A. On the back of this paper, write the steps for how to make your favorite after-school snack.

B. On another sheet of paper, write the steps for how to make your favorite snack as a how-to essay.

Oops!

Read the story. Then, write what happened next.

The children were playing baseball in the empty lot. Mischa was at bat. She swung hard and hit the ball farther than anyone else had. The ball sailed across the lot and smashed through Mrs. Avery's window. Mischa knew Mrs. Avery would be really angry. The other kids scattered. Mischa stood looking at the broken window.

_____

_____

_____

_____

_____

_____

_____

A. On the back of this paper, write about what you would have done if you were Mischa.

B. On another sheet of paper, write about a time you did something you thought you would get in trouble for.

CD-104538 • © Carson-Dellosa

What Happens Next?

Read each sentence. Write two sentences that tell two different things that could happen next.

The diver was looking at a sunken ship when he spotted a huge gray mass ahead.

_____

or

_____

Mackenzie put the cookies in the oven and called her friend Myla.

_____

or

_____

Just as he was to go on stage, Scott realized he had forgotten his lines.

_____

or

_____

 **Try This!**

A. Trade your paper with a friend. Compare your predictions and discuss which one is most likely to happen.

B. On another sheet of paper, write a story about one of the settings above.

What a View!

Use context clues to help you complete the passage using the words in the word bank.

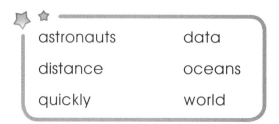

astronauts	data
distance	oceans
quickly	world

Traveling in a space shuttle is fun. The _____ can see Earth from a distance of 160 miles. Because the space shuttle orbits Earth so _____, they also see several sunrises and sunsets in one day.

They pass over continents and _____. It is very easy to see the United States and the Pacific Ocean from that _____.

The space shuttle travels around the whole _____. It takes pictures and records _____ to bring back to NASA. The journey is incredible.

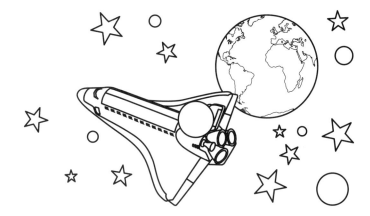

A. On the back of this paper, write a definition for each of the words in the word bank.

B: On another sheet of paper, draw a cartoon to illustrate each event in the passage above.

Fill in the Blanks

Complete the story by filling in the blanks.

A New Car

Byron had been saving his money to buy a new car. He had his heart set

on a _____,   _____,   _____.
     (describing word)   (color)   (type of car)

He went to the dealer and bought the car. Unfortunately, before leaving

the lot the _____ went _____ and the
         (part of a car)   (action)

_____ went _____.
  (part of a car)   (action)

Luckily the dealer had the car fixed, and Byron was on his way. He drove

the car to _____ first, and then he went to _____. His
      (place)   (another place)

car drove like a _____. Then, Byron took his car to _____.
        (thing)   (place)

He felt _____ of his new car.
    (feeling)

Try This!

A. Have your friend complete the story in another way. Then, compare your stories.

B. On another sheet of paper, write your own story, leaving blanks to fill in. Have a friend complete your story.

Complete the Story

Ask a friend to complete the story by filling in the blanks. Then, have your friend read the story to you, having you fill in the blanks. Count how many blanks you filled in the same as your friend.

 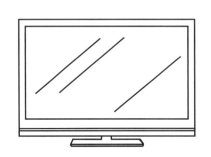 

For the Love of Movies

Hannah loved movies. She would stay up until _____ to watch them.
                                                    (time)

Her favorite characters were _____   _____ and
                              (describing word)   (type of person)

_____   _____.   One night, Hannah stayed up really late.
(describing word)   (type of person)

The next morning, when she looked into a mirror, she saw a   _____
                                                                (describing word)

_____. Hannah had turned into a character in a movie.
(type of person)

Beware! Don't stay up late watching movies, or who knows what may happen!

Try This!

A. Fill in the blanks of the story again. See if your friend can guess your responses.

B. On another sheet of paper, finish the story by telling what happened next.

What's Happening?

Read the story. Then, answer the questions.

Jack was uncomfortable. His new shirt was too stiff, and his tie felt tight. Mother had fussed over his hair, trying to get it to look just right. Finally, his mom smiled and said that Jack looked very handsome. Jack frowned. He didn't care about looking handsome.

Jack sat on the stool as he was told. He looked straight at the man his mother had hired. He didn't feel like smiling, but he did his best.

"Perfect!" said the man. "Let me get two more." Jack smiled two more times.

"That's it," said the man, "You're all done." The first thing Jack did was take off his tie!

1. What was Jack doing? _____

2. How does Jack feel about this event? _____

3. Who was the man who said, "Perfect!"? _____

4. Why did Jack take off his tie? _____

A. Underline the clues in the story that helped you answer the questions.

B. On the back of this paper, write about what you think will happen next in the story.

What Am I?

Solve the riddles.

1. Although I am clothing, don't wear me out of the house.

   What am I? _____

2. We may be light, but we keep some animals warm and dry.

   What are we? _____

3. I am good for socks and lighting a candle.

   What am I? _____

4. I am one of a kind, but I can't handle the heat.

   What am I? _____

5. Leprechauns follow me to find the pot of gold; you can find me after a summer rain.

   What am I? _____

A. On a separate sheet of paper, write five new riddles.

B. On another sheet of paper, write each riddle and list other possible answers.

CD-104538 • © Carson-Dellosa

Field Trip!

Read the story. Then, complete the organizer.

Jeremy's class was going on a field trip to the beach. They were going to see the tide pools. They were going to study the plants and the animals that lived there.

Jeremy had just moved to Los Angeles from Colorado. He had seen snow, bears, and mountains, but he had never seen the ocean. He was very excited.

The morning of the field trip, Jeremy could not get out of bed. His throat was really sore. Every time he tried to stand up, the room spun around. His mother came in to see if he was ready. When she saw him still in bed, she knew something must be wrong. She felt his forehead. He was running a fever.

"I'm not going to see the beach today, am I?" Jeremy asked.

"Not today. But, don't worry. The ocean will be there when you feel better. We will go then," his mother said.

CD-104538 • © Carson-Dellosa

Setting	Theme	Character

A. On the back of this paper, make an organizer like the one above. Then, fill out the organizer to tell about a time you went on a field trip.

B. Choose a fairy tale. On another sheet of paper, write a paragraph about its setting, character, and theme.

Book Reporter

Complete the information about a book you have read recently.

Title: _____

Author: _____

Who are the main characters? _____	Where did the story take place? _____
_____	_____
_____	_____
_____	_____
_____	_____

What were the main events in the story?

1. _____
2. _____
3. _____
4. _____

CD-104538 • © Carson-Dellosa

Try This!

A. On the back of this paper, write your own fictional story using the same characters and setting from above.

B. Write a letter to a friend explaining how to tell the difference between a fictional story and a nonfiction story.

Feature Hunt

Choose either your science or social studies textbook. Find an example of each text feature in the book. Then, write the page number where each feature is located.

Text Feature	Page Number
table of contents	
index	
glossary	
diagram	
photograph	
chart	
vocabulary word	

Try This!

A. On the back of this paper, write about which text features you use the most. Explain how each text feature is helpful.

B. Make a bookmark that reminds you to check text features every time you read.

Waterworks

Read the diagram. Number the steps, in order, to show how water is purified.

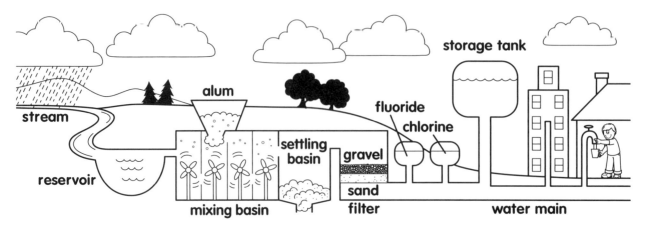

_____ The alum and dirt sink to the bottom of the settling basin.

_____ From the reservoir, water goes into a mixing basin.

_____ The clean water is stored in a large storage tank.

_____ First, raindrops fall into streams, lakes, and rivers.

_____ Water leaves the storage tank through water mains and reaches your home through your faucets.

_____ Alum is added to take the dirt out of the water.

_____ Fluoride and chlorine are added to the water.

_____ Then, the streams and rivers flow into a reservoir.

Try This!

A. On the back of this paper, write the definition of *chlorine*. Use a dictionary to help you if needed. Then, make a prediction as to why chlorine is added to water.

B. On another sheet of paper, write five questions about the diagram above. Then, have a friend answer your questions.

Flower City

Read the map. Then, answer the questions.

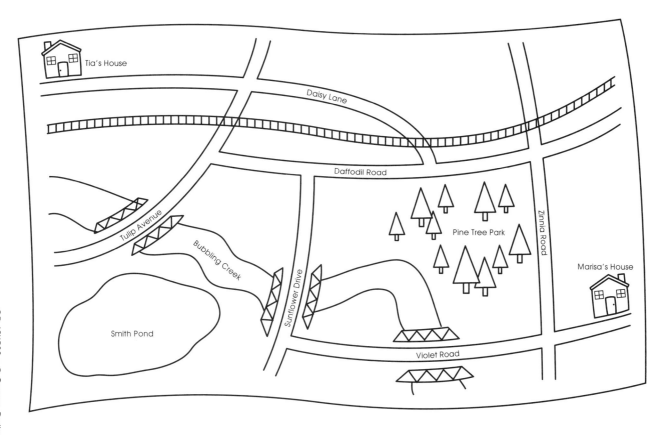

1. What three roads cross the railroad tracks? _____

2. What roads intersect both Daffodil Road and Violet Road? _____

3. How can you get across Bubbling Creek? _____

4. Give directions to get from Tia's house to Marisa's house. _____

_____

Try This!

A. On the back of this paper, write another set of directions that tell how to get from Tia's house to Marisa's house.

B. On another sheet of paper, draw and color a map of your neighborhood or an imaginary neighborhood.

Ready, Set, Draw! Part 1

Read each passage. Then, write if the passage was written to *inform* or *persuade*.

Learn to Draw!
Learn to draw COOL cartoons!

Where: 234 Art Drive

When: Saturday at noon

Who: Anyone who wants to learn!

555-1234

555-1 · 555-123 · 555-1234 · 555-1234 · 555-1234 · 555-1234

_____

M.C. Escher

Maurits Cornelis Escher was a famous artist.
He was known for his very detailed drawings.
He also used designs to create illusions such
as endless staircases and hands drawing
themselves. Escher died on March 27, 1972.

E

_____

 Try This!

A. Research more about M. C. Escher. On the back of this paper, write three more facts that could be included in the encyclopedia article.

B. On another sheet of paper, make an advertisement for art supplies that is meant to *inform*. Then, make one that is meant to *persuade*.

Ready, Set, Draw! Part 2

Read each passage. Then, write if the passage was written to *inform*, *persuade*, or *entertain*.

Dog Tails

_____

_____

 **Try This!** _____

A. On the back of this paper, create a comic strip that is meant to inform.

B. On another sheet of paper, write a newspaper article that is meant to entertain.

The Wright Brothers

Read the passage. Then, complete the organizer.

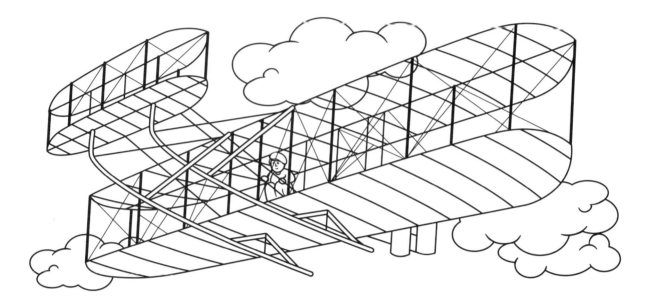

Orville and Wilbur Wright were famous American brothers. They owned a bicycle shop in Dayton, Ohio. Although they were interested in bicycles, they also loved the idea of flying. In 1896, they began to experiment, or try new ideas, with flight. They started by testing kites and then gliders, which are motor-less airplanes. These tests taught the brothers how an airplane should rise, turn, and come back to Earth. The brothers made more than 700 glider flights at Kitty Hawk in North Carolina. This was fun, but not good enough for them. Orville and Wilbur put a small engine on an airplane named Flyer I. On December 17, 1903, they took the first motor-powered flight. It lasted about one minute. The brothers continued to experiment until they could stay in the air for longer than one hour.

Who? _____

What? _____

When? _____

Where? _____

Why? _____

 **Try This!** _____

A. On the back of this paper, draw and label a picture to go with the story.

B. On another sheet of paper, draw a time line that shows the important dates from the passage.

Chirp! Chirp! Chirp!

Read each paragraph. Then, write one sentence to summarize the paragraph.

1. The baby birds were growing so quickly. Soon they would be flying. They were always hungry, so their mother flew back and forth all day long with worms and bugs for them to eat.

   _____

2. Chirpy was the smallest of the three babies. He was also the bravest. He liked to jump to the edge of the nest to see his new world. The mother bird warned him to be careful. She said that he might fall from the nest.

   _____

3. The mother bird flew away to get the babies their dinner. Chirpy hopped right up to the edge of the nest. Suddenly, his foot slipped. He began to fall. Luckily the mother bird was there to nudge him safely back into the nest.

   _____

A. On the back of this paper, write a summary of all three paragraphs.

B. On another sheet of paper, rewrite this story from Chirpy's point of view.

I Am Me

Read the poem. Then, write a summary of the poem.

I Am Me

I am unique. I am one of a kind.
My face, my body, and my mind
Are all special parts of me,
And there's no one else I'd rather be.
I like who I am. I certainly do.
I'm special to someone. I know it's true.
I am proud and happy to know
That I am ME from head to toe!

CD-104538 • © Carson-Dellosa

_____

_____

_____

_____

_____

_____

_____

_____

 **Try This!**

A. Write a song about yourself to the tune of "Row, Row, Row Your Boat."

B. On another sheet of paper, write a summary about a friend or a family member. Then, use the summary to write a poem like the one above.

Pretty Swans

Read each sentence. Write *X* in the **O** column if the sentence is an opinion. Write *X* in the **F** column if the sentence is a fact.

	O	F
1. Long ago, huge flocks of swans lived in America.		
2. Everyone loved these beautiful birds.		
3. These swans had white feathers.		
4. Swan feathers were used for writing with ink.		
5. Swan feathers were better for drawing than metal pens.		
6. A male swan is called a cob, and a female swan is called a pen.		
7. The sound a swan makes is hard on the ears.		
8. A refuge was started to protect the swans.		
9. It is wonderful to have a safe place for swans.		
10. Swans should be our national bird.		

Try This!

A. On the back of this paper, write five more facts and five more opinions about swans.

B. On another sheet of paper, draw a poster that will encourage people to save swans.

Who Said It?

Read each statement. If it is a fact, then Felipe said it. If it is an opinion, then Olivia said it. Circle the name of the person who said each statement.

1. "Eighth graders are too old to watch cartoons," complained Felipe/Olivia.

2. "A town square is part of a town," stated Felipe/Olivia.

3. "Enough rain can fall in one night to become a foot deep," explained Felipe/Olivia.

4. "Mr. Walker sells the best candy in the world," declared Felipe/Olivia.

5. "A dog is the best pet," said Felipe/Olivia.

6. "Winter is the season after autumn and before spring," stated Felipe/Olivia.

7. "Everyone likes to play in the snow," giggled Felipe/Olivia.

8. "Butter will melt on a hot pan," explained Felipe/Olivia.

CD-104538 • © Carson-Dellosa

A. What would Felipe and Olivia say about school? On the back of this paper, write five sentences that Felipe would say and five sentences that Olivia would say.

B. Look at the ads in a magazine or a newspaper. Do they have mostly facts, opinions, or a mix of both? On another sheet of paper, explain why you think this is so.

Rope Them In!

Underline the cause once and the effect twice in each sentence.

1. When the rain started, the boys ran for shelter.

2. Mother served cake after dinner because it was Malia's birthday.

3. Because I cannot swim, my dad will not let me go to the lake by myself.

4. Kevin cannot go to school because he is sick.

5. Nicole went to the movies this afternoon because she was bored.

6. I was so tired that I went to bed early last night.

7. I earned an A on my test because I studied.

8. I skinned my knee when I fell off my bike.

A. On the back of this paper, write a story about someone who is having a bad day. Use at least five cause-and-effect statements in your story.

B. On another sheet of paper, draw a poster to show the difference between cause and effect.

School Day Drama

Draw a line to connect each cause and effect.

1. Our class won the contest,

2. After our class read *Charlotte's Web*,

3. School was let out early

4. Because Jan studied hard,

5. It was raining outside,

6. Chang's alarm did not go off,

7. Our class was excited

8. Because everyone followed the rules,

A. we learned about real spiders.

B. so recess was in the gym.

C. because we were going on a field trip.

D. so we got pizza at lunch.

E. she did well on her test.

F. because of the holiday.

G. so he was late for school.

H. no one got in trouble.

CD-104538 • © Carson-Dellosa

A. On the back of this paper, make a list of other causes and effects you see at school.

B. On another sheet of paper, write a story that includes some causes and effects.

Backyard Fun

Read each sentence. Decide if the underlined portion is the cause or the effect. Color the correct answer to reveal the path to the barbeque.

1. <u>Because it was a sunny day</u>, my family had a barbeque.   (cause) (effect)

2. The food smelled good, <u>so the neighbors came over too</u>.   (cause) (effect)

3. Once the burgers finished cooking, <u>my dad put cheese on top of them</u>.   (cause) (effect)

4. <u>My brother tripped</u> and spilled his food on the ground.   (cause) (effect)

5. Because my brother spilled his food, <u>I couldn't stop laughing</u>.   (cause) (effect)

6. Everyone was smiling <u>because we were having so much fun</u>!   (cause) (effect)

7. The ants circled the picnic area <u>because they smelled food</u>.   (cause) (effect)

8. Because the sun was going down, <u>we began to light candles</u>.   (cause) (effect)

9. All of the kids were playing flashlight tag, <u>so the adults decided to play too</u>.   (cause) (effect)

10. <u>Because I had so much fun</u>, I will never forget that barbeque.   (cause) (effect)

 Try This!

A. On the back of this paper, write five more cause-and-effect sentences about the barbeque.

B. On another sheet of paper, make a poster that explains how you know if part of a sentence is the cause or the effect.

Roller Coaster Rules

Follow the directions.

1. Color all two-syllable words blue.

2. Color all three-syllable words red.

3. Color all four-syllable words green.

4. Draw a yellow box around the words that start with the letter *c*.

5. Draw an orange *X* above the words that end with the letter *e*.

6. Draw a purple line above the words that have more than one *a*.

7. Circle all of the compound words in black.

8. Draw a pink *X* after the roller coaster name that you like best.

Millennium	Corkscrew	Lightning	Thunderbolt	Anaconda
Copperhead	Avalanche	Mountain	Thrill	Flashback
Speedy	Hair-Raiser	Splash	Twisted	Backlash

Try This!

A. Create 10 more cards with a funny roller coaster name on each. Add them to your paper and follow the directions above.

B. On the back of this paper, write five steps that tell how to draw something. Have a friend follow the steps.

Missing Something?

Follow the directions to complete the picture.

1. Draw eyes on the dragonfly.

2. Draw six black spots on the ladybug.

3. Add a design to the butterfly's wings.

4. Add five yellow-and-black bees around the beehive.

5. Add two more legs to the spider.

6. Color the grasshopper green.

7. Finish coloring the rest of the picture.

Try This!

A. Draw a Venn diagram on the back of this paper. Organize the bugs from the picture on the Venn diagram. Write about how you chose to organize them.

B. On another sheet of paper, write a paragraph that describes what is happening in the picture.

Our United States

Follow the directions.

1. Write the abbreviation for your state on the state.

2. If a state is north of your state, color it blue.

3. If a state is south of your state, color it green.

4. If a state is east of your state, color it red.

5. If a state is west of your state, color it yellow.

6. Draw an *X* where four states meet at the same corner. (Hint: Four Corners in the West.)

7. Circle the two states that do not share a border with any other states.

8. Draw a star on a state that you would like to visit someday.

A. On the back of this paper, describe the route you would take to get from your state to a state you would like to visit.

B. On another sheet of paper, research a state you would like to visit. Create a travel brochure for that state.

About Frogs and Toads Part 1

Read the passage about frogs from a science book and answer the questions. Then, read the poem about frogs on page 100.

Chapter 5 Lesson 1

Frogs and Toads

Both frogs and toads are amphibians (am•**fib**•ee•uhns). Amphibians spend part of their lives as water animals and part as land animals. In the early stages of their lives, amphibians breathe through gills. When they become adults, they develop lungs. Most amphibians lay eggs near water. Both frogs and toads are born with tails that they later lose. Both have poison glands in their skin to protect them from their enemies.

Frogs and toads are different in several ways. Most toads are broader, darker, and flatter than frogs. Their skin is drier. Toads are usually covered with warts, while frogs have smooth skin. Most toads live on land, while most frogs prefer being in or near the water.

Frog

lives in or near water

smooth skin

Toad

darker

drier, bumpy skin

lives on land

---

1. Is this passage fiction or nonfiction? _____

2. What is the purpose of this passage? _____

 _____

A. On another sheet of paper, draw a poster that shows how frogs and toads are alike and how they are different.

B. On the back of this paper, write a paragraph about your favorite science subject.

About Frogs and Toads Part 2

Read the poem about frogs. Then, compare this passage with the passage about frogs on page 99.

My Frog Frank

My frog Frank is the best.
He gets to stay in my room,
even at night when it is time to rest.

My frog can hop like a rabbit,
and he can swim like a duck.
But, he does have one strange habit.

My frog Frank likes to tell jokes
about fish, bears, dogs, and toads.
Yet he hardly ever croaks.

1. Is this passage fiction or nonfiction? _____

2. What is the purpose of this passage? _____

3. Which passage would you use to learn about frogs? _____

A. On the back of this paper, draw a Venn diagram about these two passages. Tell how they are alike and how they are different.

B. Find a book about frogs. On another sheet of paper, draw a triple Venn diagram to compare the book to these two passages about frogs.

CD-104538 • © Carson-Dellosa

Planet Mercury

Read the passage about Mercury and answer the questions. Then, read about Venus on page 102 and compare.

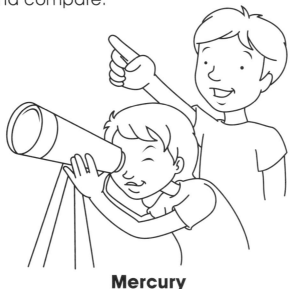

Mercury

Mercury is one of the smallest planets in our solar system. It is also the nearest planet to the sun.

Mercury spins very slowly. The side next to the sun gets very hot before it turns away from the sun. The other side freezes while away from the sun. As the planet slowly spins, the frozen side then becomes burning hot, and the hot side becomes freezing cold.

Even though Mercury spins slowly, it moves around the sun very quickly. This is why it is named Mercury, after the Roman messenger for the gods.

1. What is Mercury's position from the sun? _____

2. Would Mercury be a good place for people to live? Explain. _____

   _____

3. How did Mercury get its name? _____

A. On another sheet of paper, write a story about visiting another planet.

B. Research another planet. Write a one-page report about the planet on another sheet of paper.

Planet Venus

Read the passage about Venus. Compare this passage about Venus to the passage about Mercury on page 101.

Venus

Venus is the nearest planet to Earth. It is the second planet from the sun. Because it is the easiest planet to see in the sky, it has been called the Morning Star and the Evening Star. The Romans named Venus after their goddess of love and beauty.

Venus is covered with thick clouds. The clouds trap the sun's heat. The temperature on Venus is nearly 900°F (482°C)!

Venus turns in the opposite direction from Earth. So, on Venus, the sun rises in the west and sets in the east.

1. What is the position of Venus from the sun? _____

2. Would Venus be a good place for people to live? Explain. _____

_____

3. How did Venus get its name? _____

4. How is Venus different from Mercury? _____

 **Try This!**

A. On another sheet of paper, draw the solar system and label all of the planets.

B. On another sheet of paper, draw a Venn diagram. Complete the diagram with information about Venus and Mercury.

Name: _____

Flying Mammals

Read the passage and answer the questions. Use a crayon to underline each answer in the text in the color stated.

Bats

Bats are helpful animals. They are the only mammals that can fly. They are some of the best insect hunters. Bats use their mouths and ears to find mosquitoes, mayflies, and moths. They can eat more than a million insects in one night. They help control the insect population. Although most bats eat only insects, some eat fruit and the nectar of flowers. Bats also help flowers and spread seeds.

More than 900 different kinds of bats are in the world. Some bats are small, measuring only 1/2 inch (1.27 cm) long. Some bats are big. They can measure more than 16 inches (40.6 cm) long.

1. (yellow) How are bats helpful? _____

2. (blue) How many different kinds of bats are in the world? _____

3. (red) What do bats eat? _____

4. (green) How large can some bats get? _____

Try This!

A. On the back of this paper, explain why you think bats have such a good sense of hearing.

B. On a large sheet of paper, use a ruler to draw the size of the smallest bat and the size of the largest bat.

Nap Time

Read the passage and answer the questions.

Hibernation

Bats, chipmunks, bears, snakes, and turtles all hibernate. Hibernation is a long sleep that some animals go into for the winter.

Animals get energy from food. Some animals cannot find enough food in the winter. Instead, they eat large amounts of food in autumn. Their bodies store this food as fat. Then, in winter, they hibernate. Their bodies live on the stored fat. Because their bodies need much less food during hibernation, these animals can stay alive without eating food all winter.

1. What is hibernation? _____

   _____

2. Where do animals get their energy? _____

   _____

3. Why do some animals eat a lot of food in autumn? _____

   _____

4. Why do animals need less food during hibernation? _____

   _____

   A. On the back of this paper, draw three pictures: one of a bear before hibernation, one of a bear during hibernation, and one of a bear after hibernation.

   B. On another sheet of paper, write a story about an animal that is having trouble falling asleep during hibernation.

CD-104538 • © Carson-Dellosa

Leaning into Summer

Read the passage and answer the questions. Then, write the number of the sentence or sentences where you found each answer.

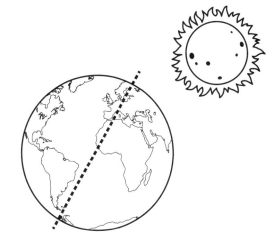

[1]Why isn't it summer all year long? [2]The seasons change because Earth is tilted like the Leaning Tower of Pisa. [3]As Earth orbits the sun, it stays tilting in the same direction in space.

[4]Let's look at the seasons in the Northern Hemisphere. [5]When the North Pole is tilting toward the sun, the days become warmer and longer. [6]It is summer. [7]Six months later, the North Pole tilts away from the sun. [8]The days become cooler and shorter. [9]It is winter.

1. Why do the seasons change?

   _____   _____ (number)

2. Describe the days when the North Pole tilts toward the sun.

   _____   _____ (number)

3. What season is it when the North Pole tilts away from the sun?

   _____   _____ (number)

4. Describe the days when the North Pole tilts away from the sun.

   _____   _____ (number)

   A. On the back of this paper, explain in your own words why we have seasons.

   B. On another sheet of paper, draw a picture of the position of Earth during winter, spring, summer, and autumn.

Busy Beavers

Read the passage and answer the questions.

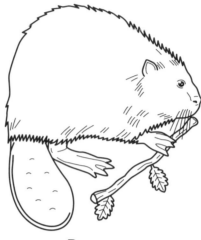

Beavers

Maybe you have heard the saying "busy as a beaver." Beavers are certainly busy animals. Beavers are good swimmers. They live around streams. They are at home on land and under water. They eat the soft inner bark of trees and bushes that grow near the water. They like aspens, birches, and willows.

Beavers build dams. Their dams help them create homes that are safe and comfortable all year long. A beaver's home is called a lodge. The entrance to the lodge is underwater, but the floor is above the waterline. The lodge has a roof of sticks and branches.

During late summer and early autumn, beavers are very busy. They store supplies of branches and sticks underwater. When winter arrives, they do not hibernate. They swim out from under the ice to get the food they have saved.

1. What do beavers eat? _____

2. Where do beavers usually live? _____

3. What is a beaver home called? _____

4. How are beavers busy animals? _____

A. Some people do not like it when beavers build dams. On the back of this paper, list some reasons why this might be the case.

B. On another sheet of paper, draw a large diagram of a beaver lodge. Draw arrows to show how the beaver gets in and out.

CD-104538 • © Carson-Dellosa

A Special Day

Read the story. Then, answer the questions by circling the answers in the text.

Last summer, Maria and Lucy won free tickets to a water park. At the park, they floated down the lazy river ride and jumped the waves in the wave pool. They even slid down the tallest waterslide in the park! The girls ate frosty snow cones and cheesy pizza. By the end of the day, they were wet and tired, but happy. It had been a great day at the water park!

1. Who is in the story? Circle your answer in the story in red.

2. Where did they go? Circle your answer in blue.

3. What four things did they do there? Circle your answers in green.

4. When did they go? Circle your answer in purple.

5. Why did they get to go there? Circle your answer in brown.

A. On the back of this paper, draw a map of the water park that Maria and Lucy went to. Use details from the story to help you.

B. Imagine that you won free tickets to an amusement park. On another sheet of paper, write an essay that describes your day.

Letter by Letter

Trace each letter five times. Use a different color of crayon each time.

Aa Bb Cc Dd Ee

Ff Gg Hh Ii Jj

Kk Ll Mm Nn

Oo Pp Qq Rr Ss

Tt Uu Vv Ww

Xx Yy Zz

Try This!

A. On the back of this paper, practice writing your name in cursive 10 times. Use a different color of crayon each time.

B. Write a note to a friend in cursive.

Name: _____

Just Jokes

Copy the joke and the answer in your best handwriting. Then, write a joke of your own.

What kind of

fish do dogs chase?

Answer: Catfish!

A. Trade papers with a friend and read each other's jokes.

B. Work with a friend to write a joke book in cursive.

Name: _Jackie   10/23/10_

On Topic

Circle the topic in each group that you think would be the easiest to write about. Cross out the topics that are too general.

1. ~~plants~~

   (cactus)

   ~~desert plants~~

2. my life

   birthdays

   (my best birthday)

3. planets

   (Mars)

   the solar system

4. board games

   games

   (how to play checkers)

5. school

   teachers

   (my favorite subject)

6. (the best ice cream flavor)

   desserts

   sweets

A. Choose one of the topics you circled above and write an essay about it on the back of this paper.

B. On another sheet of paper, write an essay about why it is important to choose a good topic when writing.

A Writing Robot

Choose a topic that you want to write about and write it in the top box. Then, complete the organizer with details about the topic.

Topic
Dancing

Detail
Dancing Salsa

Detail
Dancing in Fun

Detail
Dancing beful

Try This!

A. On the back of this paper, write a paragraph about your topic. Include the details.

B. Use the organizer to write about your favorite sport. Then, write a paragraph about your favorite sport on another sheet of paper.

That's Super!

Read the topic sentence in the large bubble and the supporting details in the small bubbles. Cross out any details that do not belong. Write additional supporting details in the empty bubbles.

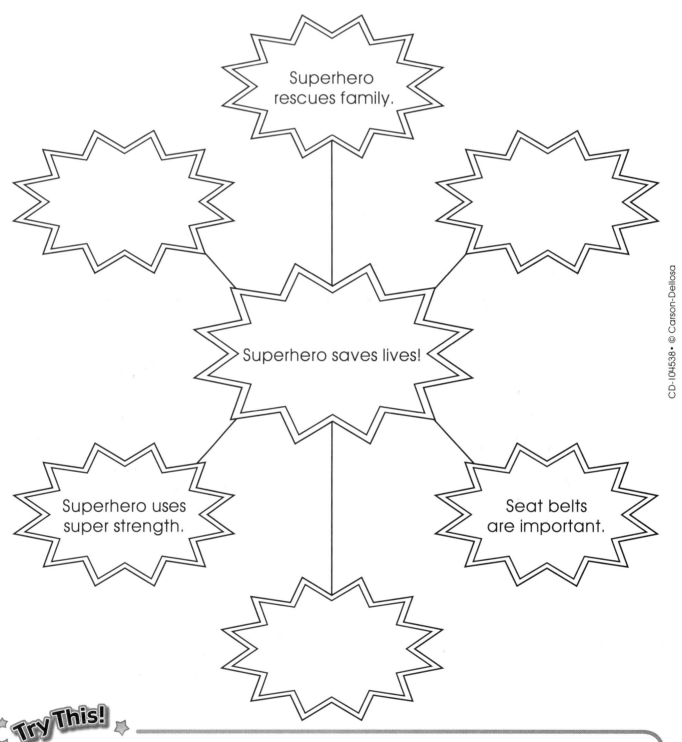

Try This!

A. On the back of this paper, write a story using the information above.

B. On another sheet of paper, make a comic strip using the information above.

For Sale

Read the advertisements. Underline the supporting details. Cross out information that is not needed.

Skateboard for Sale

Black-and-white skateboard with royal blue wheels for sale. Like new. It was my favorite board ever. I need to sell it before I can buy in-line skates. Also comes with cool stickers. Cost is $8.00. Call 555-0123.

Bike for Sale

I am selling my favorite bike. I got it for my sixth birthday. The bike is blue with white stripes. Looks like new. I took really good care of it. Comes with a light and a basket. Cost is $15.00 or best offer. Call 555-0123.

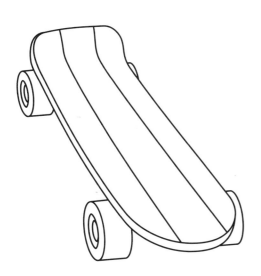

A. On the back of this paper, rewrite the advertisements, including only the important details.

B. On another sheet of paper, write an advertisement for a toy you would like to sell. Be sure to include important details.

Loose Tooth

Read the title. Complete the organizer. Then, use the outline to write a paragraph on the back of this paper.

Title: The day I lost my tooth.

Main Idea:

Supporting Details

I.

Supporting Details

2.

Supporting Details

3.

Supporting Details

4.

 **Try This!**

A. On another sheet of paper, draw a picture that shows how you lost a tooth.

B. On another sheet of paper, write a guide for other students about how to pull a loose tooth.

Wow! What a Difference!

Read the paragraph. Then, rewrite it using adjectives and more description to make it more interesting.

    Yesterday, my family took a train ride. The train had passenger cars, boxcars, and an engine. A caboose was at the end. The whistle blew. We were off! Smoke blew from the engine. The cars began to rock. I would like to ride on a train again.

_____

_____

_____

_____

_____

_____

_____

_____

_____

Try This!

A. On another sheet of paper, draw a picture to go with your train story. Include the details you added to the story in your picture.

B. On another sheet of paper, write a story about your favorite family trip. Be sure to include a lot of details and interesting descriptions.

Can You Sense It?

Write a story about something that happened in the school cafeteria. Use the organizer to help you use your senses to add details.

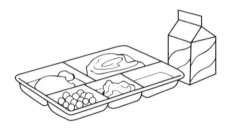

What did you see?	What did you hear?	What did you smell?

What did you taste?	What did you feel?

 **Try This!**

A. On the back of this paper, explain why you think someone who is blind usually has better senses of smell, hearing, touch, and taste.

B. On another sheet of paper, use your five senses to describe your bedroom. Then, draw a picture of your room.

Six-Legged Friends

Draw and color a picture of a one-of-a-kind insect. Then, write a descriptive paragraph telling how it looks, sounds, smells, and feels.

CD-104538 • © Carson-Dellosa

⭐ **Try This!** ⭐

A. On the back of this paper, write a story from the point of view of the insect. Be sure to include a lot of descriptive phrases.

B. On another sheet of paper, draw a picture of a real insect. Label the parts of its body. Then, write a descriptive paragraph about what each part is used for.

Colorful Phrases

Color each phrase according to the chart.

If the phrase tells . . .	then color it . . .
who	blue
what	yellow
when	green
where	red
why	orange

in the forest

worked a long time

outside

a little girl

because it was pretty

the farmer

at night

in the morning

opened the lock

to make everyone happy

 **Try This!**

A. On another sheet of paper, write a story using some of the phrases above.

B. On another sheet of paper, write a play using all of the phrases above.

Fiction vs. Nonfiction

Cut out and glue each book cover under the correct label.

Nonfiction	**vs.**	**Fiction**

✂ cut

Try This!

A. On the back of this paper, draw new book covers for a fiction and a nonfiction book above.

B. On another sheet of paper, draw a Venn diagram that compares a fiction and a nonfiction book of your choice.

119

Real or Historical?

Read each description. Then, write either *realistic fiction* or *historical fiction* on the line.

1. Anna is a young girl traveling west with her family in a covered wagon. *Out West* is a book that tells about the many adventures she and her family have along the way.

   _____

2. Andre and Melissa have been best friends since first grade. Can they still remain friends even after a new kid moves into the neighborhood? Read *Friends Forever?* to find out.

   _____

3. *Lost* is a book about the first settlers of North Carolina. A group of people came to North Carolina and lived among the Native Americans. After several months, the whole colony disappeared.

   _____

4. Kennedy Elementary School was a very fun place to be in the 1970s. Holly, Megan, and Keisha were good students. The three of them decided to start a new club at school called *The Peace Group*.

   _____

Try This!

   A. On the back of this paper, write your own book descriptions for a realistic fiction and a historical fiction book.

   B. On another sheet of paper, draw a movie poster about your favorite historical fiction book.

Do You Have a Tale?

Read each description. Then, mark an *X* in the correct box. Underline any clue words that helped you.

	Fairy Tale	**Folktale**	**Tall Tale**	**Not a Tale**
1. Ella was always treated badly by her sisters. Then one day, her fairy godmother showed up to help her out.	☐	☐	☐	☐
2. Three little birds lived in the same tree. Every day, a big, bad cat watches them. The birds try to outsmart the cat.	☐	☐	☐	☐
3. Jake and Jared liked to play jokes on people. They were the class clowns.	☐	☐	☐	☐
4. Cindy was searching for prince charming. No matter how many frogs she kissed, she just could not find him.	☐	☐	☐	☐
5. A long time ago, a boy named John tried to defeat a giant with only a stick and a stone.	☐	☐	☐	☐

Try This!

A. On the back of this paper, explain the difference between a tall tale and a fairy tale.

B. On another sheet of paper, draw a book cover for each of the books described above.

The New Kid

Read the journal entries. Then, answer the questions.

August 12

I can't believe my parents made me move to this new town. It's so unfair! Nobody asked me if I wanted to move. I don't see why my dad couldn't just find a new job in our old town. Sometimes, I really think they just do stuff like this to make me miserable! Now, I have to go to a new school where I don't know anybody. Maybe I'll just pretend to be sick tomorrow so I won't have to go.

August 13

Well, my new school is not so bad. I met a new friend who is really nice. He lives just down the street. My teacher is really cool. Her name is Ms. Panetta. She is young and really funny. She even has a pet snake in our classroom. Today, we got to do a fun art project using colored pencils. I guess moving here isn't so bad after all.

CD-104538 • © Carson-Dellosa

1. How is the writer feeling on August 12? Underline examples in the text.

_____

2. How did the writer's feelings change on August 13? Underline examples in the text. _____

3. Is the writing in this journal formal or friendly? Provide examples to support your answer. _____

_____

 **Try This!**

A. On another sheet of paper, write a journal entry about a time when you were unhappy and something cheered you up.

B. On another sheet of paper, make a chart that compares you to the character in the journal entry. How are you alike? How are you different?

Name: _____

Birthday Surprise!

Read the passage. Cross out any boring words or phrases. Then, add some exciting details.

My last birthday was neat. When I woke up, my mom made me breakfast. I opened some presents. I got some neat stuff. Then, I got dressed and went to school. Someone left a birthday present on my desk. I was happy. I opened it. A neat gift was inside! Then, my friends started singing a birthday song to me. I have good friends. I will never forget that birthday. It was the best ever!

A. On the back of this paper, draw a picture of your favorite birthday gift. Around the picture, write different words to describe the gift.

B. On another sheet of paper, rewrite this story from the point of view of one of the friends.

CD-104538 • © Carson-Dellosa

123

What Did You Say?

Write some phrases that different people might say.

A phrase my teacher might say: _____

_____

A phrase my friend might say: _____

_____

A phrase my neighbor might say: _____

_____

A phrase a parent might say: _____

_____

A phrase an older brother might say: _____

_____

CD-104538 • © Carson-Dellosa

A. On the back of this paper, make a list of phrases your best friend says. Then, write a story in your friend's voice.

B. On another sheet of paper, write five things that you say. Then, write a story that includes those phrases.

They Win!

Read each situation. Then, write a sentence that the person might say. Be sure to use quotation marks and correct punctuation.

1. Ava's team just won the championship soccer game.

_____

2. Ava's dad is proud of the way she played the game.

_____

3. Ava's brother is happy for his sister.

_____

4. Ava's best friend likes the trophy.

_____

5. Ava feels very happy.

_____

A. On the back of this paper, write a newspaper article telling about a championship soccer game.

B. On another sheet of paper, write a story about Ava winning the championship soccer game. Include some of the dialogue that you wrote above.

Movie Matters

Imagine that you and a friend are deciding what movie to see. Write the conversation below.

You: _____

Friend: _____

You: _____

Friend: _____

You: _____

Friend: _____

You: _____

Friend: _____

CD-104538 • © Carson-Dellosa

A. Think of your favorite movie. On another sheet of paper, write something that your favorite character says in the movie.

B. On another sheet of paper, write a dialogue between three friends trying to decide what movie to see.

Name: _____

It's a Dog's Life

Write a story about the dog's day using transition words such as *first, then, next, after,* and *finally.*

_____

_____

_____

_____

_____

_____

_____

_____

_____

_____

A. On the back of this paper, draw a picture of what was happening with the dog right before your story started. Then, draw a picture of what happens to the dog after your story ends.

B. On another sheet of paper, write a story about a boy and his dog. Use transition words.

I Could Never . . .

Think of something that you would never do. Write it in the center square.
Then, complete the graphic organizer about the topic you chose.

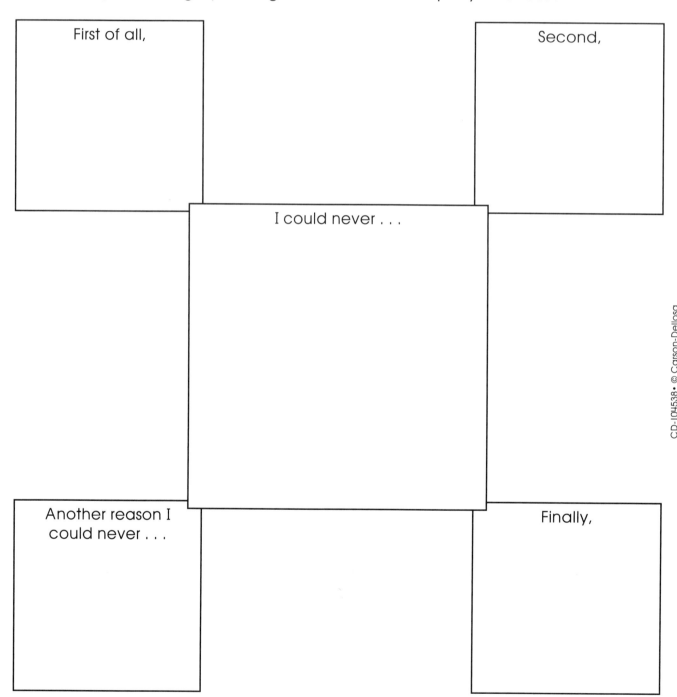

First of all,

Second,

I could never . . .

Another reason I
could never . . .

Finally,

 Try This!

A. Write a letter to a parent or a friend convincing him or her to stop a bad habit. Be sure to give good reasons in your letter.

B. On another sheet of paper, use the organizer to help you write a paragraph to tell about something you would never do.

Camping Fun

Read the paragraph. Find and correct the 18 errors.

Camping can be so much fun last weekend, me and my family went camping

in a park near the mountins. We took lots of stuff because we weren't sure what

we would need. Dad and I set up the tents, while Mom and my brother built a

campfire and make lunch. After lunch, we went swimming in the lake. Later,

we went fishing my dad cot five fish! He cleaned it and cooked them over the

campfire for diner. They tasted grate! After dinner, we tosted marshmallows and

tell scary storys. I wasn't really afraid. Finally, we crawled inside our tents to go to

sleep. It was quite except for the crickets. The next morning, we got up and starts

another day of fun. I love camping?

Try This!

A. On another sheet of paper, write your own camping story. Be sure to check for spelling errors.

B. Create a brochure for a campsite near the Grand Canyon.

A Great Year

Read the paragraph. Find and correct the 22 errors.

Last year was alot of fun. In january, we went skiing in denver Colorado. In

february, my class performed a play about the life of martin Luther king, jr. I got

to play the part of dr king. In the spring, my family spent a weak at the beech.

We seen two baby sharks swiming around the fishing pier! During the summer, I

visited my Grandparents in Texas. I visited the space center in houston. Finally,

in december, I had the best birthday ever! I got a puppy. I named him wolf

because he looks like a baby wolf. Last year was relly a lot of fun. I hope next

year will be even better!

Try This!

A. On another sheet of paper, write about a favorite thing you did with your family last year.

B. On another sheet of paper, write a rule to explain each mistake you corrected in the paragraph.

Amazing Autumn

Read the paragraph. Use proofreaders' marks to correct any mistakes.

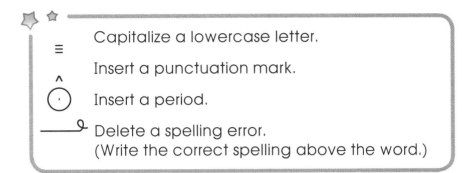

≡   Capitalize a lowercase letter.

∧   Insert a punctuation mark.

⊙   Insert a period.

⌇   Delete a spelling error.
     (Write the correct spelling above the word.)

Autumn is my favorite time of year. in september,

the leaves begin to change colors and it starts to get

chilly at night my dog, ranger, likes to jump in the piles

of leafes. mom makes hot chocolate to take to the

football game we like to watch the team from central

high school they are the red raiders. go red raiders it is time for the pumpkin harvest

in october Do you like pumpkins my little sister thinks they are funny looking. In

november, we drive into the town of Evansville becauze they have a big parade my

uncle bob lets my sister sit on his shoulders so that she can

see everything. She is so lucky that's OK becauze I always

get to have the first piece of pie at diner. i hope you can

see why I like autumn. what is your favorate season

A. Trade papers with a friend. Compare your editing changes. Make any additional
changes that the two of you feel are needed.

B. On another sheet of paper, write about your favorite season.

My Little Brother

Read the paragraph. Find and correct the errors.

My little brother makes me crazy! why did I even have to have a brother. He only

causes trobble he cries breaks things and runs after the dog. Our house was quiet

when he wasnt around. But, he does made me laugh. Like the time he was chaseing

the dog, and the dog stoped and started to chase him. He laughed and laughed.

That kid has a grate laugh. Are hole family was laughing. I gess he is fun sometimes I

also like to read storys to him. He thinks I'm really smart I guess that kid isn't so bad. I

just wish he wasnt so loud when I'm trying to right a papper.

A. On the back of this paper, list the types of errors you found in the paragraph.

B. On another sheet of paper, write about one of your family members.

Dear Friend

Use the organizer to write a letter to a friend. Then, rewrite the letter on another sheet of paper.

_____
(date)

_____
(greeting)

_____

_____

_____

_____

_____

_____
(closing)

_____
(signature)

 **Try This!**

A. On another sheet of paper, make a colorful poster labeling the different parts of a letter.

B. What letter-writing rules would stay the same when writing an e-mail to a friend? What rules would change? Write your answers on another sheet of paper.

Dear Pen Pal

Imagine that you have a pen pal in another state. Use the organizer to write a letter to your pen pal. Then, rewrite the letter on another sheet of paper.

_____
(date)

_____
(greeting)

_____

_____

_____

_____

_____

_____
(closing)

_____
(signature)

A. On another sheet of paper, write a letter to a friend. Tell her what you are learning in school.

B. On another sheet of paper, write a second letter to a pen pal. Tell him or her about your school and your friends.

Please Send

Address the envelope from you to your friend. Draw a stamp.

_____

_____

_____

                              _____

                              _____

                              _____

 Try This!

A. Make a poster that explains the three parts of addressing an envelope correctly.

B. Correctly address an envelope from you to a family member. Then, write a letter to that family member and mail it.

Dinosaur Descriptions

Complete each list with words that describe dinosaurs. Then, use the words to write a descriptive paragraph about a dinosaur. Use the back of this paper if needed.

Nouns	Verbs	Adjectives
tail	stomp	huge
teeth	graze	spiked
_____	_____	_____
_____	_____	_____
_____	_____	_____

_____

_____

_____

_____

_____

_____

_____

Try This!

A. Research a dinosaur. Then, write a descriptive paragraph about it on another sheet of paper.

B. On another sheet of paper, write a story that explains how dinosaurs became extinct. Use a lot of descriptive words and phrases.

Take Your Pick

Circle one item in each list. Then, write a descriptive paragraph about the words you circled. Use the back of this paper if needed.

List 1	List 2	List 3
hamster	running	at the zoo
leopard	hiding	in the bathtub
bear	stuck	under the car
parrot	sleeping	in your desk
cricket	talking	on TV

_____

_____

_____

_____

_____

_____

_____

_____

_____

CD-104538 • © Carson-Dellosa

Try This!

A. Reread the paragraph you wrote. Add more description using your five senses—sight, hearing, touch, taste, and smell. Rewrite the paragraph on another sheet of paper.

B. Draw a picture of your favorite after-school snack. Write a descriptive paragraph about it on another sheet of paper.

On the Moon

Write a descriptive paragraph about a visit to the moon.

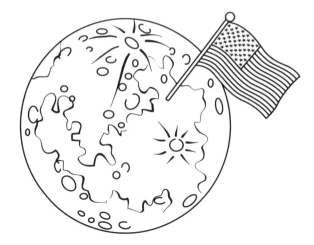

_____
_____
_____
_____
_____
_____
_____
_____
_____
_____

A. On another sheet of paper, write a descriptive paragraph about a visit to another planet.

B. Research the moon. On another sheet of paper, write a report that describes what the moon looks like and include some scientific facts about it.

Friends Forever

Complete the organizer. Then, use it to write a story about friends on the back of this paper.

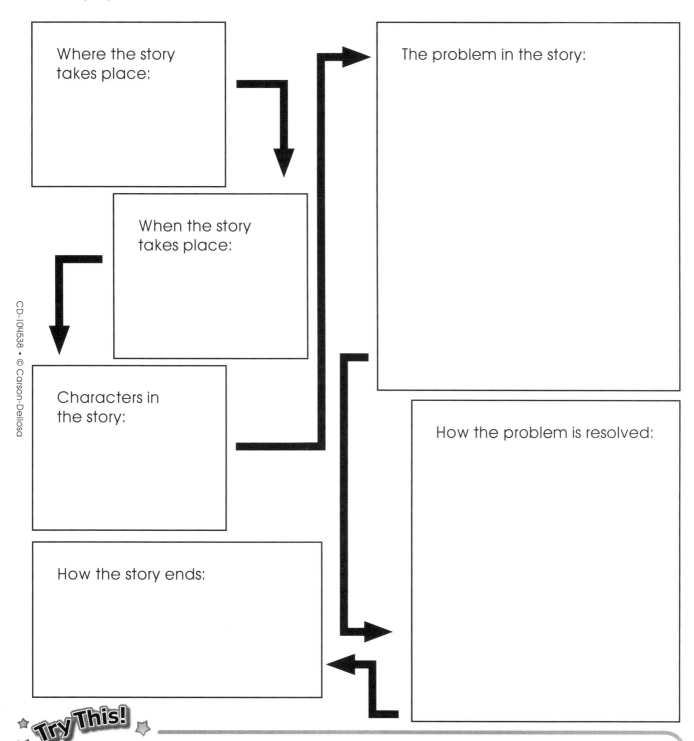

Where the story takes place:

When the story takes place:

Characters in the story:

How the story ends:

The problem in the story:

How the problem is resolved:

CD-104538 • © Carson-Dellosa

Try This!

A. List all of the things you look for in a friend. Then, write a paragraph on another sheet of paper explaining why these things are important to you.

B. Create another organizer like the one above on another sheet of paper. Write a story about friends in another setting or place in time.

A School Story

Cut out the cards below. Choose one Who, What, When, Where, and Why card and write a story using those details.

Who?	Who?	Who?
a third-grade teacher and the principal	five students	the librarian and a cafeteria worker

What?	What?	What?
notice strange things happening	are suddenly very happy	disappeared

When?	When?	Where?
before school	after school	in the hallways

Why?	Why?	Why?
in the classroom	no one knows	because it was Saturday

cut ✂

CD-104538 • © Carson-Dellosa

A. Trade stories with a friend. Edit each other's work.

B. Write two more cards for *Who, What, When, Where,* and *Why.* Organize the cards by type and choose one card from each type. On another sheet of paper, write another story using the new cards.

The Princess to the Rescue

Read the beginning of the fairy tale. Then, write two different solutions to the problem.

The princess had come to save the prince who was trapped in a deep hole.
The princess brought only a rope, a rock, and a bucket of sand.

Solution 1	Solution 2

A. Choose one of the solutions and write the complete fairy tale.

B. Rewrite the fairy tale from the point of view of the princess or the prince.

Story Starters

Choose one of the story starters and use it to write a narrative on another sheet of paper.

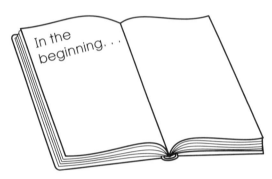

Yesterday, I got the worst haircut.
Last Saturday, I went shopping with my mother, and I got lost.
The poor kitten had been stuck in the tree for hours.
It was the summer between third grade and fourth grade, and my family moved to a new house.
I won a huge trophy.
The soccer game was tough.
My alarm did not go off.
I told the best joke to my friend.
Last weekend, I spent the night at my friend's house.
I know I saw the man in that painting move.

 **Try This!**

A. On the back of this paper, draw a picture to illustrate your narrative.

B. Choose another story starter and write another narrative on another sheet of paper.

Problems Solved!

Choose one of the problems. Write an expository paragraph explaining how you would solve the problem. Use the back of this paper if needed.

Problem 1	**Problem 2**	**Problem 3**
how to keep from being late	how to remember to bring necessary supplies to school	how to keep track of homework assignments

_____

_____

_____

_____

_____

_____

_____

_____

A. Write a paragraph that explains a problem you had and how you solved it.

B. Many inventions were created out of a need to solve a problem. On another sheet of paper, draw a picture of an invention you think might help solve one of the problems above.

143

Frozen Yogurt Treat

Write an expository paragraph that explains how to make your favorite frozen yogurt treat. Then, color the yogurt treat as you like it.

_____

_____

_____

_____

_____

_____

_____

_____

A. On the back of this paper, draw a picture of your favorite frozen yogurt treat.

B. On another sheet of paper, write a recipe for your frozen yogurt treat.

CD-104538 • © Carson-Dellosa

Classroom Rules

Complete the organizer with information about your classroom rules. Then, on another sheet of paper, use the information to a write a letter to a future student explaining how to do well in this class.

Classroom Rules:	Things you SHOULD NOT do in class:
	Things you SHOULD do in class:

Other tips to succeed:

CD-104538 • © Carson-Dellosa

 **Try This!**

A. On another sheet of paper, create a poster stating the classroom rules.

B. On another sheet of paper, write a paragraph that explains what you think next year will be like and how you can be successful.

Pretty Please?

Write three reasons why your teacher should not assign homework. Then, on another sheet of paper, write a persuasive paragraph that includes the three reasons.

Reason 1:

_____

_____

Reason 2:

_____

_____

Reason 3:

_____

_____

A. On another sheet of paper, write a response you think your teacher would give to your persuasive paragraph.

B. On another sheet of paper, write a persuasive paragraph trying to get someone to do something that you want.

CD-104538 • © Carson-Dellosa

Two Sides to Everything

Complete the organizer to respond to the question. Then, choose a side and write a persuasive paragraph on another sheet of paper.

Should students go to school year-round?

For	Against

A. On another sheet of paper, write a persuasive paragraph for the other side of the argument.

B. On another sheet of paper, rewrite your paragraph as a letter to your principal.

Laughable Limericks

Follow the pattern to write a limerick.

Limerick

A silly poem with five lines that tells a story.

The last words in lines 1, 2, and 5 rhyme.

The last words in lines 3 and 4 rhyme.

Example:

There once was a girl in third grade

who loved to sip lemonade.

She drank it all day

and then went to play

while drinking the 'ade she had made.

CD-104538 • © Carson-Dellosa

_____

_____

_____

_____

_____

Try This!

A. On another sheet of paper, write another limerick and illustrate it.

B. Find a poem and practice reading it. Then, read the poem aloud to the class.

Celebrating Cinquains

Follow the pattern to write a cinquain.

Cinquain

A poem with five lines shaped like a diamond

Line 1: a noun

Line 2: two adjectives describing the noun

Line 3: three *-ing* verbs describing the noun

Line 4: a phrase or a sentence about the noun

Line 5: a synonym for the noun

Example:

Big Dipper

beautiful, bright

shining, glittering, sparkling

home to the North Star

constellation

_____

_____

_____

_____

CD-104538 • © Carson-Dellosa

A. Rewrite your cinquain neatly on another sheet of paper. Draw and color a picture to illustrate it.

B. Write a poem about the stars, the moon, or the sun. Share it with a friend.

Dropping Digits

Write the digits 0–9 to answer the problems. Do not repeat digits within an answer.

1. The number that is closest to but not more than 30. _____

2. The smallest 3-digit number with all odd digits. _____

3. The number with 7 tens and 0 ones. _____

4. The greatest 3-digit number with all even digits. _____

5. The greatest 3-digit number with all odd digits. _____

6. The number that is 1 more than 323. _____

7. The number that is 10 more than 50. _____

8. The number that is 1 more than 17. _____

 Try This!

A. Write the numbers 1–100 on a sheet of grid paper. Write the digits 0–9 on the first row and 10–19 on the second row. Continue the pattern to 100.

B. On the back of this paper, write four of your own problems similar to the ones above. Give them to a friend or a family member to solve.

CD-104538 • © Carson-Dellosa

Spaghetti with Meatballs

Draw a noodle from each number in the first column to show the correct place value.

1. 752

A. three hundreds eight tens eight ones

2. 509

B. six hundreds two tens three ones

3. 388

C. four hundreds nine tens two ones

4. 623

D. nine hundreds one ten two ones

5. 110

E. seven hundreds five tens two ones

6. 492

F. five hundreds four tens seven ones

7. 876

G. five hundreds nine ones

8. 912

H. eight hundreds seven tens six ones

9. 547

I. one hundred one ten

10. 650

J. six hundreds five tens

CD-104538 • © Carson-Dellosa

 Try This!

A. On the back of this paper, write five other 3-digit numbers and the place value of each.

B. Find a book with more than 100 pages, randomly open the book, and write the page numbers you open to in words.

Place Value Places

Complete the chart.

Place Value Chart

	thousands	hundreds	tens	ones
1. ninety-one				
2. 1,000 + 900 + 80 + 9				
3. 3,514				
4. 4,000 + 300 + 20 +1				
5. three hundred six				
6. 1,000 + 20 + 3				
7. one thousand eight				
8. 9,150				
9. 6,000 + 100 + 3				
10. two thousand seventy				

A. On another sheet of paper, draw a fun and colorful place value chart to keep at your desk and use when you need it.

B. On another sheet of paper, use some of the numbers from above to write a narrative story about space.

Place Value Puzzle

Write each number in the puzzle.

Across

1. 3 thousands, 5 hundreds, 9 ones
3. eight thousand seven hundred fifty-four
5. one hundred sixty-two
7. seven hundred eighty-two
9. 2 hundreds, 5 tens
10. 5 ten thousands, 1 thousand, 3 hundreds, 2 tens, 4 ones
12. two
13. nine thousand six hundred four
15. seven hundred
16. eight
17. 6 ten thousands, 6 thousands, 4 hundreds, 8 tens

Down

1. three thousand seven hundred seventy-nine
2. ninety-one
3. 8 tens, 2 ones
4. 5 hundreds, 8 tens, 5 ones
6. six hundred seventy-three
8. twenty-five
9. twenty-four thousand six hundred seventy-four
11. 2 tens, 9 ones
12. two thousand one
14. four thousand
16. 8 hundreds, 6 tens, 1 one

Try This!

A. Color each digit in the ten thousands place yellow.

B. On another sheet of paper, make your own place value puzzle for a friend to solve.

Race to the Finish

Complete the chart.

Place Value Chart

	ten thousands	thousands	hundreds	tens	ones
1. fifty thousand two hundred twenty-five					
2. ninety-nine thousand nine hundred ninety-nine					
3. sixty thousand four hundred thirty-seven					
4. fifty-six thousand two hundred two					
5. seven thousand four hundred sixty					
6. nineteen thousand three					
7. four thousand three hundred fifty-one					
8. sixty-eight thousand fifty-seven					

A. On the back of this paper, write the number that is 10 less than each number above.

B. On the back of this paper, write the number that is 100 more than each number above.

Step on In!

Look at the Venn diagram. Answer the questions using the numbers in the diagram. Then, label each circle correctly.

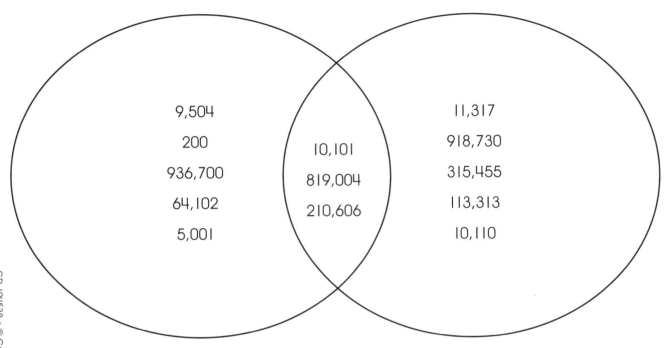

9,504
200
936,700
64,102
5,001

10,101
819,004
210,606

11,317
918,730
315,455
113,313
10,110

1. Write the largest number. _____

2. Write the smallest number. _____

3. Write the 5-digit number whose digit in the ten thousands place is equal to 60,000. _____

4. Write the number between 250,000 and 350,000. _____

5. Write an odd number less than 300,000 but more than 100,000. _____

6. Write an even number between 9,000 and 10,000. _____

A. On the back of this paper, write the numbers in order from smallest to largest.

B. On the back of this paper, write five more questions that can be answered using the numbers in the Venn diagram.

Numbers in Disguise Part 1

Write each number. Then, circle the number in the puzzle on page 157.

1. 9,000 + 800 + 50 + 1= _____

2. 4,000 + 200 + 5 = _____

3. 5,000 + 40 + 4 = _____

4. 3,000 + 100 + 70 = _____

5. 2,000 + 300 + 40 + 5 = _____

6. five thousand three hundred twenty-seven _____

7. four thousand three hundred sixty-seven _____

8. thirty-six thousand seven hundred forty-three _____

9. ten thousand sixty-seven _____

10. five thousand eight hundred nine _____

A. Circle three more numbers in the puzzle on page 157. Write those numbers in words and expanded form on the back of this paper.

B. On another sheet of paper, write a mystery story. Include several numbers in your story that are written in different forms.

CD-104538 • © Carson-Dellosa

Numbers in Disguise Part 2

Circle your numbers from page 156 in the puzzle. Numbers can be found going across and down.

⭐ **Try This!** ⭐

A. Find three more numbers in the puzzle and write them in them in words and expanded form on the back of this paper.

B. On another sheet of paper, explain the differences between writing numbers in standard form, words, and expanded form.

Write It Out

Write each number in words.

1. 763 _____

2. 1,019 _____

3. 7,517 _____

4. 4,102 _____

5. 467 _____

6. 54,399 _____

7. 11,111 _____

8. 23,057 _____

A. On the back of this paper, write four different numbers. Then, write each number in word form.

B. On the back of this paper, rewrite the numbers in order from least to greatest.

CD-104538 • © Carson-Dellosa

There's No Comparison

Write >, <, or = to compare each pair of numbers. Circle the letter next to the greater number. If the numbers are equal, circle both letters. To solve the riddle, write the circled letters in order on the answer lines.

1. **T** 759 ( ) 258 **S**
2. **H** 161 ( ) 161 **E**
3. **B** 25 ( ) 29 **Y**
4. **B** 230 ( ) 320 **A**
5. **R** 685 ( ) 594 **M**
6. **E** 267 ( ) 267 **S**
7. **M** 141 ( ) 139 **B**
8. **A** 342 ( ) 324 **B**
9. **M** 573 ( ) 753 **R**
10. **L** 206 ( ) 208 **T**
11. **K** 882 ( ) 822 **D**
12. **I** 425 ( ) 254 **S**
13. **A** 330 ( ) 338 **D**
14. **N** 980 ( ) 995 **S**

Why do baby goats know how to compare numbers?

Answer: Because ___ ___ ___ ___   ___ ___ ___

___ ___ ___ ___ ___ ___   " ___ ___ ___ ___ "

⭐ **Try This!** ⭐

A. Write a paragraph about a time when you had to compare two numbers.

B. Make a list of activities that involve comparing numbers.

Compare Numbers

Write >, <, or = to compare each pair of numbers.

1. 620 ◯ 6,200

2. 493 ◯ 439

3. 6,432 ◯ 16,408

4. 9,286 ◯ 13,489

5. 724 ◯ 724

6. 3,080 ◯ 3,800

7. 9,876 ◯ 9,887

8. 10,001 ◯ 10,001

9. 45,015 ◯ 45,016

10. 7,999 ◯ 79,099

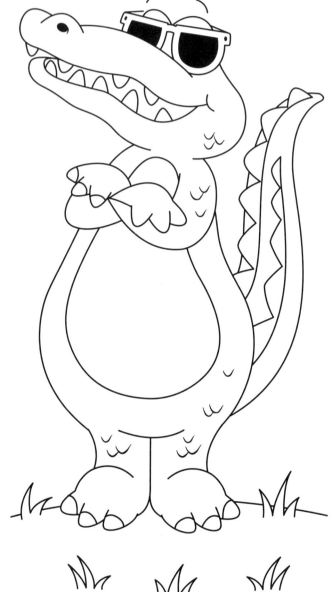

Try This!

A. Choose 10 numbers from this page. On the back of this paper, write each number in word form. Then, write each number in expanded form.

B. Make a poster that explains how to compare numbers. Be sure to use the words *greater than*, *less than*, and *equal to*.

Compare Cards

Cut out the cards. Place them facedown. Draw two cards and write a comparison sentence using >, <, or = to show how the numbers compare.

698	406	54,374	2,473
546	5,678	96,589	725
608	758	6,409	57,234
2,164	810	2,362	21,056
473	968	4,596	58,740

 cut

Try This!

A. Shuffle the cards and repeat the game, creating 10 new comparison sentences.

B. Order all of the number cards from smallest to largest.

Spin! Spin! Spin!

For each problem, use a paper clip and a pencil to spin the spinner. Write the symbol for what was spun in the oval. Then, write a number to make the comparison true.

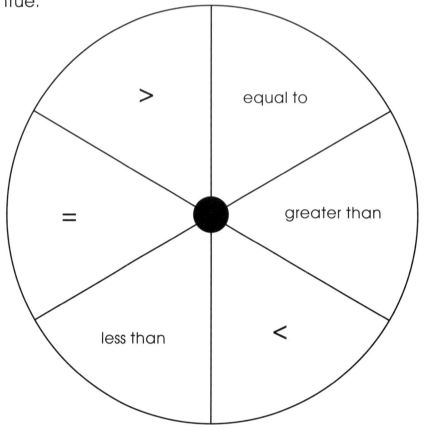

1. 573 ⬭ _____

2. 57,483 ⬭ _____

3. 4,736 ⬭ _____

4. 353 ⬭ _____

5. 3,575 ⬭ _____

6. 43,743 ⬭ _____

7. 7,968 ⬭ _____

8. 342 ⬭ _____

A. Spin the spinner. Write five comparisons to match the spin. Spin the spinner again and write five more comparisons to match that spin.

B. On the back of this paper, list five different situations in which you might need to compare numbers.

Stack Them Up

Write the numbers in order in the place value chart. Begin with the largest number on the bottom and end with the smallest number on top.

hundreds	tens	ones

120

938

234

905

869

570

403

296

586

506

A. On the back of this paper, write the numbers in expanded form.

B. On the back of this paper, explain in words how to compare the numbers 14,586 and 14,485.

163

Lay the Bricks

Cut out the bricks and glue them on the wall in order from largest to smallest starting at the bottom right. Follow the arrows.

4,374	39,213	79,890	30,967	4,403
1,383	65,860	2,131	59,340	43,405
4,586	70,958	9,487	3,085	

Try This!

A. Look around your classroom. Write 20 numbers that you find in order from least to greatest.

B. On the back of this paper, make a place value chart that includes ones, tens, hundreds, thousands, and ten thousands. Write each number above in the place value chart.

Rainbow Numbers

For each set of numbers, write the largest number in red. Write the second-largest number in orange. Write the third-largest number in green and the fourth-largest number in blue.

1. 5,732 921 1,240 932

_____

2. 9,834 5,685 960 4,723

_____

3. 753 4,323 1,238 1,423

_____

4. 235 3,486 8,560 4,086

_____

5. 3,483 301 235 2,463

_____

6. 4,967 3,023 2,139 587

_____

7. 932 4,672 3,984 2,164

_____

8. 256 1,236 3,710 396

_____

9. 355 6,150 9,325 4,356

_____

10. 2,356 823 908 6,346

_____

CD-104538 • © Carson-Dellosa

A. On the back of this paper, list some reasons why it is important to know place value.

B. Find 10 numbers in a newspaper or magazine. On another sheet of paper, write them in order from least to greatest.

Windstorm!

Write the missing digits to make each set of numbers ordered from least to greatest.

1. 11,091   11,[ ]32   11,225

2. 1[ ],432   [ ]3,011   1[ ],009

3. 54,7[ ]6   5[ ],786   54,[ ]89

4. 88,903   88,9[ ]3   88,[ ]23

5. 4,[ ]78   [ ],460   4,[ ]60

6. 2[ ],921   [ ]6,001   26,[ ]50

7. 4,[ ]37   4,7[ ]5   4,73[ ]

8. 5,[ ]11   5,11[ ]   5,113

A. On the back of this paper, order each set of numbers from greatest to least.

B. On another sheet of paper, order all of the numbers from least to greatest.

CD-104538 • © Carson-Dellosa

Name: _____

Every Dog Has Its Day

Round each number to the nearest ten. Match each answer with the correct letter in the key. To solve the riddle, write the letters in order on the answer lines.

1. 594 _____
2. 455 _____
3. 1,723 _____
4. 2,787 _____
5. 7,865 _____
6. 879 _____
7. 342 _____
8. 3,954 _____
9. 1,698 _____
10. 776 _____

340 = O	
460 = H	
590 = S	
780 = E	
880 = O	
1,700 = L	
1,720 = A	
2,790 = M	
3,950 = D	
7,870 = P	

What kind of dog likes to take a bath?

Answer: A " ___ ___ ___ ___ – ___ ___ ___ ___ ___ ___ "

Round each number to the nearest hundred. Match each answer with the correct letter in the key. To solve the riddle, write the letters in order on the answer lines.

11. 886 _____
12. 842 _____
13. 657 _____
14. 3,179 _____
15. 1,920 _____
16. 6,059 _____
17. 4,846 _____

700 = L	
800 = U	
900 = B	
1,900 = D	
3,200 = L	
4,800 = G	
6,100 = O	

What kind of dog chases red objects?

Answer: A " ___ ___ ___ ___ – ___ ___ ___ "

A. Draw a picture of a dog. Use the code above to write a name for your dog.

B. Explain to a friend the best way to round numbers. Use another sheet of paper to help you.

Fishy Addition

Add. Remember to regroup if needed. Use the code to color the fish.

green = 96 and 74

orange = 73 and 82

red = 35 and 52

yellow = 92 and 51

blue = 77

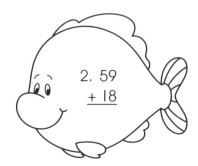

1. 28
+ 54

2. 59
+ 18

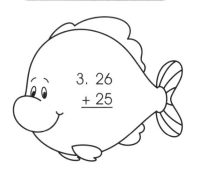

3. 26
+ 25

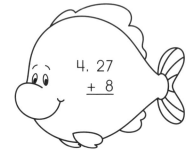

4. 27
+ 8

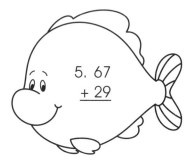

5. 67
+ 29

6. 16
+ 36

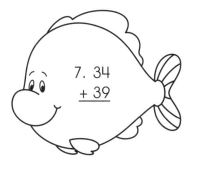

7. 34
+ 39

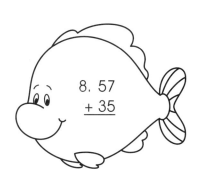

8. 57
+ 35

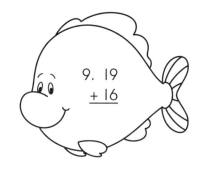

9. 19
+ 16

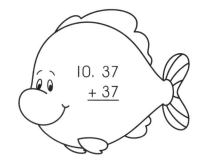

10. 37
+ 37

 **Try This!**

A. Use a calculator to check your answers. Correct any incorrect answers.

B. On the back of this paper, write three more addition problems that have the same answer as three of the fish above. Use the code to color the fish.

Name: _____

Domino Addition

Add. Regroup if needed.

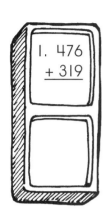
1. 476
+ 319

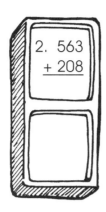
2. 563
+ 208

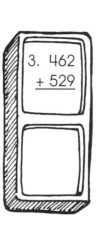
3. 462
+ 529

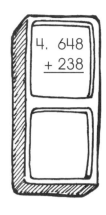
4. 648
+ 238

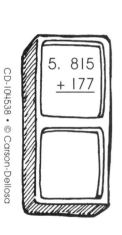
5. 815
+ 177

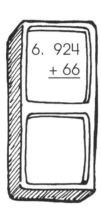
6. 924
+ 66

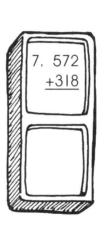
7. 572
+ 318

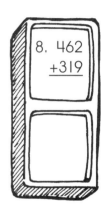
8. 462
+ 319

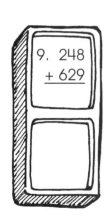
9. 248
+ 629

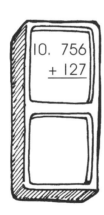
10. 756
+ 127

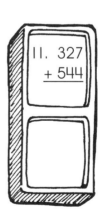
11. 327
+ 544

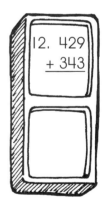
12. 429
+ 343

Try This!

A. Create 10 more dominoes on another sheet of paper. Cut out all of the dominoes and play a game with them.

B. On another sheet of paper, explain how you know if a number needs to be regrouped.

Old Glory

Add. Regroup if needed. Then, solve the riddle by writing the letter that matches each answer in the correct space below.

What do the 13 stripes on the U.S. flag stand for?

1. 371 + 439	3. 146 + 587	5. 347 + 328	7. 327 + 649	9. 283 + 519
T	**R**	**H**	**E**	**C**
2. 629 + 184	4. 264 + 483	6. 382 + 249	8. 283 + 636	10. 423 + 392
O	**I**	**S**	**N**	**L**

810	675	747	733	810	976	976	919

802	813	815	813	919	747	976	631

A. On another sheet of paper, draw the United States flag. In each stripe, write and solve an addition problem.

B. Research the names of the 13 colonies. Write them on the back of this paper.

Name: _____

Top of the Pile

Add. Regroup if needed.

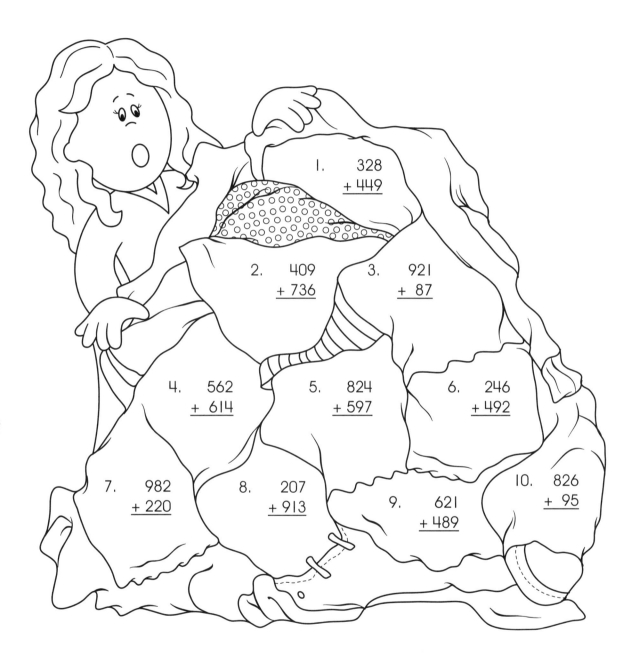

1. 328
    + 449

2. 409
    + 736

3. 921
    + 87

4. 562
    + 614

5. 824
    + 597

6. 246
    + 492

7. 982
    + 220

8. 207
    + 913

9. 621
    + 489

10. 826
    + 95

CD-104538 • © Carson-Dellosa

A. Write your answers in order from least to greatest.

B. Write five more 3-digit addition problems and solve them.

171

Strike!

Add each pair of numbers to complete each set of bowling pins.

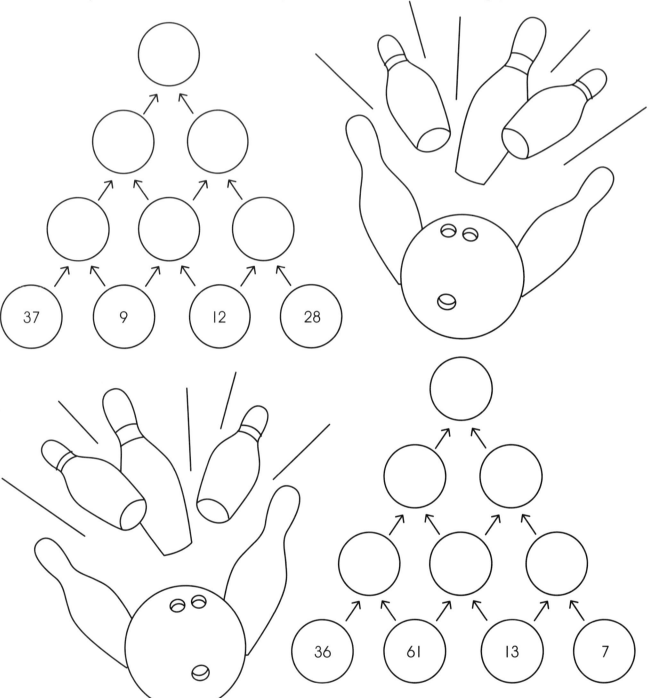

37   9   12   28

36   61   13   7

A. On another sheet of paper, write all of the addition problems above.
For example, 37 + 9 = 46. You should have 12 problems.

B. On another sheet of paper, create and solve your own problems like the ones above.

Estimation Organization

Cut out the problems. Estimate the answers and glue the problems in order from the least sum to the greatest sum. Then, solve the problems to see how you did.

1. 2,641 + 6,259	2. 8,465 + 1,386	3. 6,843 + 2,391
4. 6,241 + 2,363	5. 5,942 + 1,829	6. 5,642 + 2,919
7. 2,648 + 1,923	8. 4,826 + 2,098	9. 5,642 + 319

CD-104538 • © Carson-Dellosa

cut

Try This!

A. On another sheet of paper, write five new addition problems that have sums greater than the greatest sum above.

B. Write about how you estimated each problem.

What a Web!

Solve each problem. Write the numbers of the problems that have differences of 12 in the web.

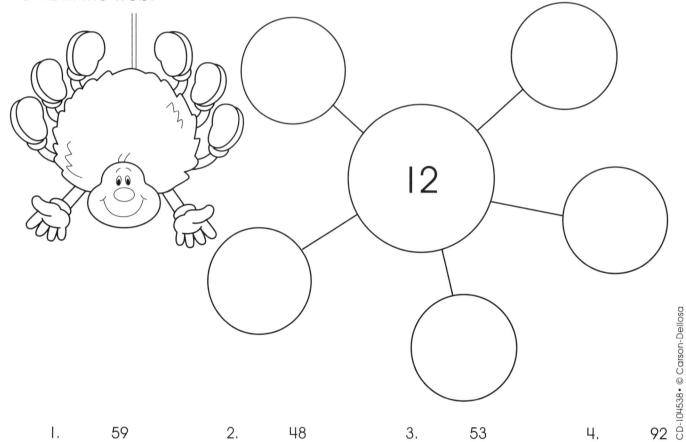

1.	59 − 47	2.	48 − 26	3.	53 −41	4.	92 − 60
5.	44 − 32	6.	89 − 75	7.	67 − 55	8.	85 − 73

A. Create a new web with the number 15 in the center. Write five subtraction problems, each with the difference of 15.

B. Create a new web with the number 172 in the center. Write five subtraction problems, each with the difference of 172.

CD-104538 • © Carson-Dellosa

Name: _____

Subtraction Superhero

Subtract. Regroup as needed.

1.
```
  570
- 458
```

2.
```
  383
- 273
```

3.
```
  359
- 259
```

4.
```
  359
- 257
```

5.
```
  446
- 327
```

6.
```
  953
- 839
```

7.
```
  774
- 658
```

8.
```
  384
- 279
```

9.
```
  190
-  89
```

10.
```
  575
- 471
```

11.
```
  493
- 386
```

12.
```
  751
- 638
```

13.
```
  696
- 576
```

14.
```
  590
- 487
```

15.
```
  585
- 476
```

16.
```
  372
- 134
```

A. On the back of this paper, use addition to check your answers above.

B. On another sheet of paper, write a story about a subtraction superhero. Be sure to include solving subtraction problems as one of the superhero's greatest strengths.

Sub-track-tion

Subtract. Regroup as needed.

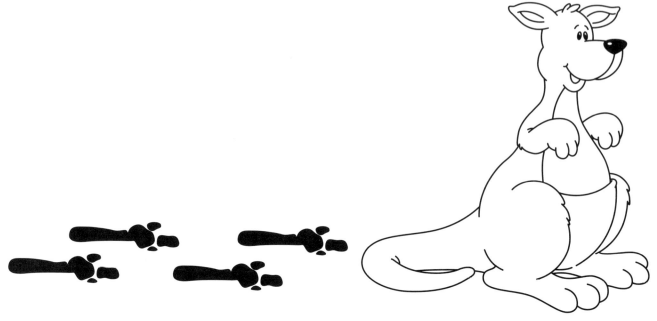

1.	348 − 153	2.	765 − 673	3.	427 − 382	4.	568 − 475
5.	637 − 446	6.	878 − 697	7.	548 − 363	8.	748 − 483
9.	824 − 653	10.	439 − 256	11.	447 − 373	12.	543 − 382
13.	484 − 364	14.	896 − 135	15.	642 − 462	16.	529 − 373

CD-104538 • © Carson-Dellosa

A. On the back of this paper, use addition to check your answers above.

B. Make a poster that explains how to do the subtraction problem 524 − 378.

Tic-Tac-Toe

Subtract. Regroup as needed. Draw a line through the row that has all of the same answers.

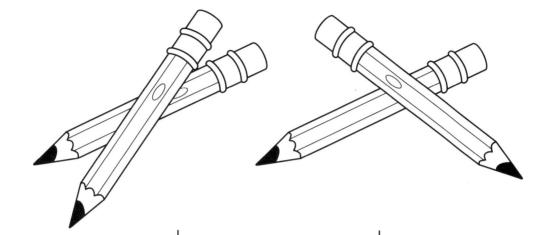

1.   542
    − 383
	2. 638
	    − 453
		3. 478
		    − 336

4.   737
    − 448
	5. 313
	    − 154
		6. 567
		    − 384

7.   984
    − 643
	8. 468
	    − 399
		9. 501
		    − 342

 **Try This!**

A. On the back of this paper, use addition to check your answers above.

B. On the back of this paper, create a new tic-tac-toe board with subtraction problems. Play tic-tac-toe with a friend.

Name: _____

Round and Round

Subtract. Regroup as needed. Write your answer in the circle. The last digit of your answer will be the first digit of the next answer.

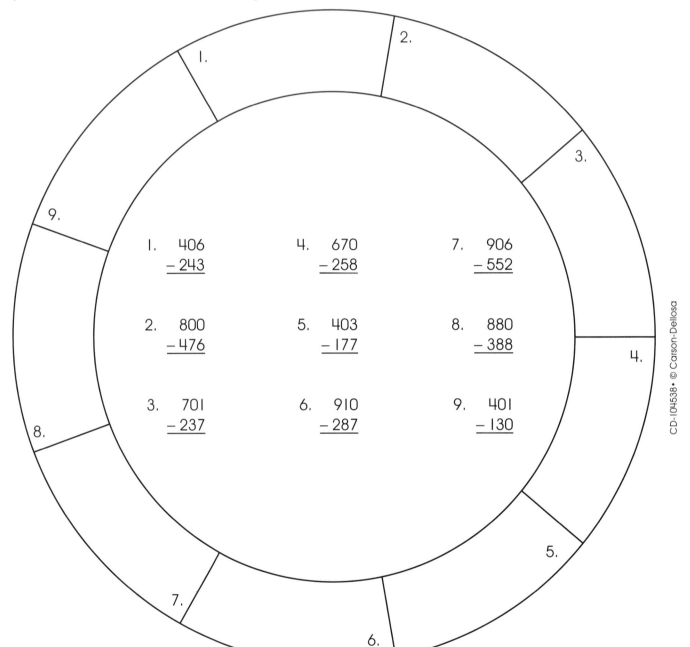

1. 406 − 243
2. 800 − 476
3. 701 − 237
4. 670 − 258
5. 403 − 177
6. 910 − 287
7. 906 − 552
8. 880 − 388
9. 401 − 130

CD-104538 • © Carson-Dellosa

A. Write five more 3-digit subtraction problems. Include at least one 0 in each number.

B. Write two new problems for the activity above. Make sure that the last digit of the answer is the first digit of the next problem's answer.

It's a Puzzler!

Add or subtract to solve the puzzle.

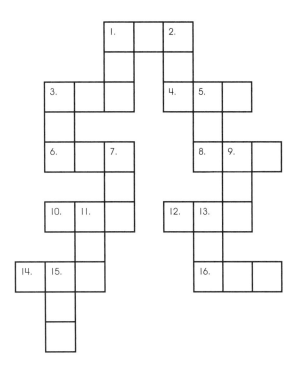

Across

1. 413 + 312

3. 102 + 415

4. 223 + 103

6. 131 + 253

8. 324 + 321

10. 207 + 222

12. 105 + 214

14. 315 + 400

16. 121 + 503

Down

1. 859 – 112

2. 985 – 402

3. 887 – 344

5. 789 – 583

7. 699 – 240

9. 589 – 100

11. 767 – 512

13. 497 – 321

15. 259 – 151

Try This!

A. On another sheet of paper, solve the above problems. Show your work.

B. On another sheet of paper, write new addition and subtraction problems that could be used to solve this puzzle.

Estimation Station

Estimate each sum or difference to the greatest place value. Circle the correct answer.

1.   27
     + 14

   A. 41   B. 40
   C. 50   D. 51

2.   34
     − 28

   A. 0   B. 10
   C. 20   D. 12

3.   59
     + 14

   A. 50   B. 70
   C. 73   D. 55

4.   92
     − 56

   A. 40   B. 36
   C. 30   D. 20

5.   72
     + 68

   A. 100   B. 0
   C. 20   D. 140

6.   62
     − 48

   A. 10   B. 14
   C. 20   D. 24

7.   162
     + 89

   A. 23   B. 250
   C. 15   D. 13

8.   251
     − 143

   A. 100   B. 300
   C. 200   D. 250

 **Try This!**

A. On the back of this paper, find the exact answer for each problem above.

B. On the back of this paper, write five new addition and subtraction problems. Estimate each answer. Then, find each exact answer.

Trucking Through Addition

Use the digits 3, 5, 7, or 9 to make each problem correct.

1. 836 + [ ]0 = 926

2. 362 + 4[ ] = 409

3. 368 + [ ]29 = 897

4. 374 + 3[ ][ ] = 773

5. 8[ ]5 + 552 = 1,387

6. 4,768 + 2,8[ ]4 = 7,662

7. 4,50[ ] + 2,[ ]43 = 7,250

8. 4,[ ]67 + [ ],571 = 7,938

9. 1,84[ ] + 6,7[ ]2 = 8,595

 **Try This!**

A. On the back of this paper, explain the strategy you used to find the missing digit in each problem.

B. On another sheet of paper, write a letter to your teacher to explain how you solved the problems.

Stagecoach Code

Use inverse operations to find each missing subtrahend. Then, complete the code key.

1.
```
   5 6 4 8
 - * # * •
 ─────────
   3 2 2 3
```

2.
```
   * ☺ # ▲
 -   8 2 5
 ─────────
   1 3 2 3
```

3.
```
   7 6 4 1
 - • * # □
 ─────────
   2 3 9 5
```

4.
```
   7 6 4 8
 - ○ * ▲ ▼
 ─────────
   4 3 5 9
```

5.
```
   • # ♦ ▲
 - 1 2 9 1
 ─────────
   4 1 1 7
```

6.
```
   ▲ * ♦ ▼
 - 4 1 8 2
 ─────────
   4 0 2 7
```

7.
```
   8 4 1 9
 - * ☺ ▲ *
 ─────────
   6 2 3 7
```

8.
```
   □ * # ▼
 - 1 5 2 6
 ─────────
   4 7 2 3
```

9.
```
   □ # * ▲
 - 4 1 5 9
 ─────────
   2 2 6 9
```

Code Key

*	▲	#	♦	•	☺	□	▼	○

 **Try This!**

A. On another sheet of paper, rewrite all of the problems using numbers in place of the symbols. Use a calculator to check your answers.

B. On the back of this paper, create your own code and problems. Have a friend solve the problems and crack your code.

CD-104538 • © Carson-Dellosa

Alphabet Unknowns

Replace each letter with a number to make the problem correct.

$a = ?, b = ?,$ and $x = ?$

CD-104538 • © Carson-Dellosa

1. $a + 7 = 12$

   $a =$ _____

2. $x + 9 = 14$

   $x =$ _____

3. $s - 12 = 6$

   $s =$ _____

4. $8 + k = 18$

   $k =$ _____

5. $21 + n = 29$

   $n =$ _____

6. $t + 9 = 34$

   $t =$ _____

7. $51 - a = 12$

   $a =$ _____

8. $y + 13 = 25$

   $y =$ _____

9. $548 - x = 123$

   $x =$ _____

10. $b - 245 = 461$

    $b =$ _____

A. Write a sentence that explains what a variable means in math.

B. On another sheet of paper, write 10 more problems using a variable. Then, solve for
each variable.

Puzzling

Use the numbers in the box to make each number sentence true if $a = 12$ and $x = 15$.

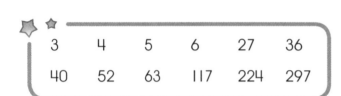

3	4	5	6	27	36
40	52	63	117	224	297

1. $a +$ _____ $= 48$

2. $7 +$ _____ $= a$

3. $52 - a =$ _____

4. $a - 8 =$ _____

5. $75 -$ _____ $= a$

6. $x -$ _____ $= a$

7. $67 -$ _____ $= x$

8. $9 +$ _____ $= x$

9. $x +$ _____ $= 312$

10. _____ $- x = a$

11. _____ $+ x = 132$

12. $239 - x =$ _____

A. On the back of this paper, write how you solved the first five problems.

B. On the back of this paper, write 10 true number sentences with $a = 3$ and $x = 9$.

CD-104538 • © Carson-Dellosa

Name: _____

Variables

On a Roll

Write an expression with variables to help you solve each problem.

1. Mario had some marbles.
   He gave 23 marbles away.
   He had 53 marbles left. How many
   marbles did he start with?

2. Mario and his friend have a total
   of 27 red marbles. If his friend has
   18 red marbles, how many red
   marbles does Mario have?

3. Mario had 52 blue marbles.
   After he went to the store, he had
   twice as many blue marbles as he
   had before. How many blue
   marbles did he have after he
   went to the store?

4. Mario and a friend had a total
   of 36 marbles. Mario had 12
   marbles. How many marbles did his
   friend have?

A. On the back of this paper, write your own word problem about Mario and his marbles.
Then, challenge a friend to solve it.

B. On another sheet of paper, make a poster that explains what a variable is.

CD-104538 • © Carson-Dellosa

185

Seeing Dots

Draw a line to match each multiplication problem with its picture.

1. 3 x 7 = 21

2. 5 x 5 = 25

3. 4 x 3 = 12

4. 2 x 9 = 18

5. 6 x 4 = 24

6. 3 x 5 = 15

7. 5 x 7 = 35

8. 6 x 6 = 36

A. •••••
•••••
•••••

B. •••
•••
•••
•••

C. •••••••••••
•••••••••••

D. ••••••••
••••••••
••••••••

E. ••••••••
••••••••
••••••••
••••••••
••••••••

F. •••••
•••••
•••••
•••••
•••••

G. ••••••
••••••
••••••
••••••
••••••
••••••

H. •••••
•••••
•••••
•••••
•••••

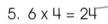

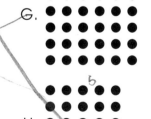

Try This!

A. On the back of this paper, show 5 x 8 and 6 x 9 using dots.

B. On the back of this paper, write eight more multiplication problems. Then, use dots to show each problem.

Hidden Problems

Find the 16 problems hidden in the puzzle. Circle the numbers across each row from left to right that make true multiplication problems. Then, add × and = to make each sentence true. An example has been done for you.

2	5	(3	× 7	= 2	1)	3	5	0	6	9
4	6	2	4	3	9	6	3	1	8	7
5	3	1	7	8	4	3	2	2	1	2
6	5	3	0	3	3	9	2	3	6	7
1	2	3	4	1	2	8	5	4	0	6
0	3	9	2	7	3	5	6	1	6	9
3	8	2	4	4	7	2	8	5	5	4
5	3	1	5	7	5	3	5	1	4	4

CD-104538 • © Carson-Dellosa

A. On the back of this paper, write the 16 multiplication problems you found in the puzzle.

B. On another sheet of paper, create a hidden puzzle like the one on this page for a friend to solve.

Name: _____

Top Secret

Solve each problem. Below each answer, write the letter from the code that matches. Read the coded question and write the answer in the space provided.

40	35	32	63	42	56	49	48	81	36	54	72
E	G	H	I	N	O	S	T	U	W	X	Y

9 x 4	8 x 4	7 x 8

7 x 9	7 x 7

7 x 7	9 x 7	8 x 6	6 x 8	7 x 9	6 x 7	7 x 5

7 x 6	8 x 5	9 x 6	6 x 8

8 x 6	8 x 7

9 x 8	7 x 8	9 x 9

?

Answer: _____

A. On another sheet of paper, create your own secret code using multiplication problems. Then, write a secret message for a friend to solve.

B. Using the same code, write a letter to your teacher on the back of this paper. See if your teacher can crack the code.

Practice Makes Perfect 1 to 6

Solve the multiplication problems. Then, cut out the cards and use them to study the multiplication facts.

1

1 x 1 = 1
2 x 1 = 2
3 x 1 = 3
4 x 1 = 4
5 x 1 = 5
6 x 1 = 6
7 x 1 = 7
8 x 1 = 8
9 x 1 = 9
10 x 1 = 10
11 x 1 = 11
12 x 1 = 12

3

1 x 3 = 3
2 x 3 = 6
3 x 3 = 9
4 x 3 = 12
5 x 3 = 15
6 x 3 = 18
7 x 3 = 21
8 x 3 = 24
9 x 3 = 27
10 x 3 = 30
11 x 3 = 33
12 x 3 = 36

5

1 x 5 = 5
2 x 5 = 10
3 x 5 = 15
4 x 5 = 20
5 x 5 = 25
6 x 5 = 30
7 x 5 = 35
8 x 5 = 40
9 x 5 = 45
10 x 5 = 50
11 x 5 = 55
12 x 5 = 60

2

1 x 2 = 2
2 x 2 = 4
3 x 2 = 6
4 x 2 = 8
5 x 2 = 10
6 x 2 = 12
7 x 2 = 14
8 x 2 = 16
9 x 2 = 18
10 x 2 = 20
11 x 2 = 22
12 x 2 = 24

4

1 x 4 = 4
2 x 4 = 8
3 x 4 = 12
4 x 4 = 16
5 x 4 = 20
6 x 4 = 24
7 x 4 = 28
8 x 4 = 32
9 x 4 = 36
10 x 4 = 40
11 x 4 = 44
12 x 4 = 48

6

1 x 6 = 6
2 x 6 = 12
3 x 6 = 18
4 x 6 = 24
5 x 6 = 30
6 x 6 = 36
7 x 6 = 42
8 x 6 = 48
9 x 6 = 54
10 x 6 = 60
11 x 6 = 66
12 x 6 = 72

cut

Try This!

A. Have a friend or a family member quiz you on the multiplication facts. On another sheet of paper, write each fact you missed 10 times.

B. Time yourself to see how fast you can complete the multiplication facts on this page.

Practice Makes Perfect 7 to 12

Solve the multiplication problems. Then, cut out the cards and use them to study the multiplication facts.

7	9	11
1 x 7 = _____	1 x 9 = _____	1 x 11 = _____
2 x 7 = _____	2 x 9 = _____	2 x 11 = _____
3 x 7 = _____	3 x 9 = _____	3 x 11 = _____
4 x 7 = _____	4 x 9 = _____	4 x 11 = _____
5 x 7 = _____	5 x 9 = _____	5 x 11 = _____
6 x 7 = _____	6 x 9 = _____	6 x 11 = _____
7 x 7 = _____	7 x 9 = _____	7 x 11 = _____
8 x 7 = _____	8 x 9 = _____	8 x 11 = _____
9 x 7 = _____	9 x 9 = _____	9 x 11 = _____
10 x 7 = _____	10 x 9 = _____	10 x 11 = _____
11 x 7 = _____	11 x 9 = _____	11 x 11 = _____
12 x 7 = _____	12 x 9 = _____	12 x 11 = _____

8	10	12
1 x 8 = _____	1 x 10 = _____	1 x 12 = _____
2 x 8 = _____	2 x 10 = _____	2 x 12 = _____
3 x 8 = _____	3 x 10 = _____	3 x 12 = _____
4 x 8 = _____	4 x 10 = _____	4 x 12 = _____
5 x 8 = _____	5 x 10 = _____	5 x 12 = _____
6 x 8 = _____	6 x 10 = _____	6 x 12 = _____
7 x 8 = _____	7 x 10 = _____	7 x 12 = _____
8 x 8 = _____	8 x 10 = _____	8 x 12 = _____
9 x 8 = _____	9 x 10 = _____	9 x 12 = _____
10 x 8 = _____	10 x 10 = _____	10 x 12 = _____
11 x 8 = _____	11 x 10 = _____	11 x 12 = _____
12 x 8 = _____	12 x 10 = _____	12 x 12 = _____

CD-104538 • © Carson-Dellosa

 cut

 Try This!

A. Circle the multiplication facts that you know. Write the facts that you need to practice 10 times each.

B. Did you know that the digits of the product of nine times any single digit number equals nine? For example, 4 x 9 = 36. 3 + 6 = 9. On another sheet of paper, write about other tricks you know from learning the multiplication facts.

Name: _____

On the Farm

Solve the problems.

1. Three horses are running in a field. How many legs are there in all?

   _____ horses with _____ legs each = _____ legs in all.

2. Five spiders are building webs in the barn. How many legs are there in all?

   _____ spiders with _____ legs each = _____ legs in all.

3. Two grasshoppers are hiding in the grass. How many legs are there in the grass?

   _____ grasshoppers with _____ legs each = _____ legs in all.

4. Four 3-legged milking stools are in the barn. How many legs are there in all?

   _____ stools with _____ legs each = _____ legs in all.

5. Six cows are eating grass on the hill. How many legs are there in all?

   _____ cows with _____ legs each = _____ legs in all.

6. Seven hens are laying eggs. How many legs are there in all?

   _____ hens with _____ legs each = _____ in all.

A. Write a number sentence for each problem above.

B. On the back of this paper, write five new word problems using multiplication on the farm.

Down the Slide

Solve the multiplication problems.

1.	92 x 2		5.	11 x 9		9.	33 x 3
2.	43 x 2		6.	31 x 4		10.	12 x 4
3.	23 x 3		7.	42 x 2		11.	31 x 5
4.	10 x 8		8.	21 x 7		12.	31 x 6

 **Try This!**

A. On another sheet of paper, write word problems for five of the problems above.

B. On another sheet of paper, make a poster that explains the steps to solve two-digit multiplication problems.

On Top of Spaghetti

Solve the problems. Then, cut out each matching answer and glue it in the space provided.

1. There are 21 plates of spaghetti. There are 4 meatballs on top of each plate. How many meatballs are there in all?

2. Three people order plates of spaghetti each day for 33 days. How many plates of spaghetti did they order in 33 days?

3. It takes 23 pounds of spaghetti noodles to feed a group of people. Two groups of people just ordered spaghetti. How many pounds of noodles need to be cooked?

4. Alex loves spaghetti. He eats it 42 times a year. How many times will Alex eat spaghetti in 3 years?

Try This!

A. On the back of this paper, explain how to multiply two-digit numbers.

B. On another sheet of paper, draw a picture of spaghetti with meatballs. Under the picture, write your own multiplication word problem to go with the picture.

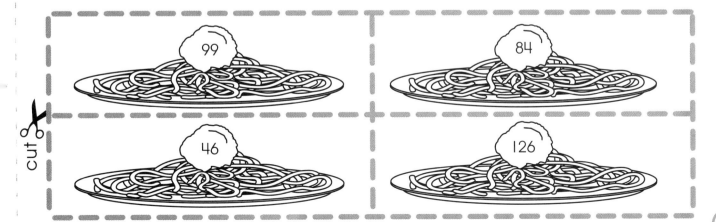

99   84

46   126

CD-104538 • © Carson-Dellosa

Name: _____

Blown Away!

Use the digits 0, 1, 2, 3, 4, 5, 6, 7, 8, and 9 to complete the multiplication problems.

1.

2	7
x	▨
5	4

2.

▨	4
x	6
8	4

3.

3	▨
x	2
7	6

4.

2	5
x	▨
7	5

5.

	3	3
	x	▨
1	3	2

6.

	1	2
	x	9
1	▨	8

7.

	2	2
	x	8
1	7	▨

8.

	3	2
	x	▨
1	6	0

9.

	1	▨
	x	9
1	7	1

10.

	2	2
	x	▨
1	5	4

⭐ **Try This!** ⭐

A. On the back of this paper, explain what you think is the hardest part about multiplying with regrouping. Then, explain what you think is the easiest part.

B. On another sheet of paper, write a word problem that uses two-digit multiplication with regrouping. Challenge a friend to solve it.

Disco Dancing

Multiply. When you need to regroup, be sure to carry the number in the disco ball.

1. 52	2. 32	3. 19	4. 44	5. 27
x 6	x 7	x 2	x 3	x 5

6. 17	7. 55	8. 38	9. 29	10. 73
x 2	x 5	x 4	x 2	x 9

11. 23	12. 48	13. 62	14. 82
x 7	x 4	x 6	x 8

 Try This!

A. Compare your answers with a friend's answers. For every answer you both have the same, give yourself a star. For every answer that is different, redo the problem to find the right answer.

B. Choose one multiplication problem from above. Write a word problem about it on the back of this paper.

Name: _____

Saddle Up!

Solve each problem. Cross out the matching answer. Not all answers will be used.

1. Sally rounds up 98 cattle each day for one week. How many cattle does she round up in all?

2. Sally needs to place 74 bales of hay in each pasture. Her family owns 6 different pastures with 12 animals in each. How many bales of hay does she need to place in the pastures in all?

686   444   132
118   923   457

3. One horse eats 2 pounds of food a day. If Sally has 59 horses on her ranch, how many pounds of food does she need to feed them each day?

4. In one week, Sally rides 33 miles. How many miles does she ride each month?

 **Try This!**

A. On the back of this paper, write two more multiplication word problems about Sally using the problems 47 x 8 and 39 x 7.

B. On another sheet of paper, explain to a friend how to multiply two-digit numbers by one-digit numbers.

Fun with Fleas

Draw a line to match each division problem with its picture.

1. $8 \div 2 = 4$

2. $16 \div 4 = 4$

3. $24 \div 8 = 3$

4. $36 \div 6 = 6$

5. $42 \div 6 = 7$

6. $35 \div 7 = 5$

7. $18 \div 3 = 6$

8. $28 \div 7 = 4$

A.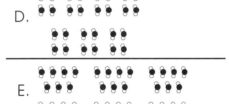

B.

C.

D.

E.

F.

G.

H.

Try This!

A. On the back of this paper, write five more problems and pictures to show each problem above.

B. On another sheet of paper, write a multiplication problem using the numbers in the problems above. For example, $8 \div 2 = 4$ can be written $2 \times 4 = 8$.

Yours and Mine

With a partner, solve the problems on each side of the page.

1. 4)‾12‾	1. 8)‾56‾
2. 12)‾48‾	2. 2)‾18‾
3. 11)‾77‾	3. 4)‾24‾
4. 7)‾14‾	4. 7)‾49‾
5. 2)‾20‾	5. 1)‾8‾
6. 9)‾63‾	6. 5)‾15‾
7. 8)‾24‾	7. 8)‾48‾
8. 5)‾45‾	8. 5)‾25‾
9. 1)‾11‾	9. 3)‾9‾
10. 9)‾27‾	10. 7)‾35‾
11. 6)‾18‾	11. 6)‾42‾
12. 10)‾120‾	12. 9)‾72‾
13. 3)‾21‾	13. 10)‾90‾
14. 11)‾88‾	14. 12)‾60‾

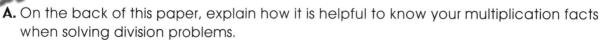

 Try This!

A. On the back of this paper, explain how it is helpful to know your multiplication facts when solving division problems.

B. On another sheet of paper, write a story about the boy on the page and how he likes to divide things into *yours* and *mine*.

We Are Family

Complete the equations.

$12 \div 3 =$ __4__	$24 \div 6 =$ __4__ R2	$28 \div 7 =$ __4__
$12 \div 4 =$ __3__	$24 \div 4 =$ __6__	$28 \div 4 =$ __7__
$3 \times 4 =$ __12__	$6 \times 4 =$ __24__	$7 \times 4 =$ __28__
$4 \times 3 =$ __12__	$4 \times 6 =$ __24__	$4 \times 7 =$ __28__
$36 \div 9 =$ __4__	$40 \div 8 =$ __5__	$63 \div 7 =$ __9__
$36 \div 4 =$ __9__	$40 \div 5 =$ __8__	$63 \div 9 =$ __7__
$9 \times 4 =$ __36__	$8 \times 5 =$ __40__	$7 \times 9 =$ __63__
$4 \times 9 =$ __36__	$5 \times 8 =$ __40__	$9 \times 7 =$ __63__
$35 \div 7 =$ __5__	$54 \div 6 =$ __9__	$32 \div 8 =$ __4__
$35 \div 5 =$ __7__	$54 \div 9 =$ __6__	$32 \div 4 =$ __8__
$7 \times 5 =$ __35__	$9 \times 6 =$ __54__	$8 \times 4 =$ __32__
$5 \times 7 =$ __35__	$6 \times 9 =$ __54__	$4 \times 8 =$ __32__

A. Write a fact family using the numbers 7, 6, and 42.

B. Write five more fact families on the back of this paper.

Hot Magma Math

Solve the division problems.

1. $4\overline{)24}$

2. $7\overline{)42}$

3. $2\overline{)14}$

4. $3\overline{)15}$

5. $9\overline{)72}$

6. $6\overline{)24}$

7. $5\overline{)45}$

8. $4\overline{)28}$

9. $6\overline{)54}$

10. $8\overline{)48}$

11. $7\overline{)49}$

12. $9\overline{)63}$

13. $5\overline{)25}$

14. $8\overline{)24}$

15. $8\overline{)64}$

16. $6\overline{)30}$

17. $6\overline{)36}$

18. $8\overline{)56}$

19. $9\overline{)81}$

20. $7\overline{)35}$

Try This!

A. Make flash cards of division facts that are hard to remember. Practice the facts.

B. On the back of this paper, write five word problems using some of the division facts above.

Building Fences

Solve the problems. Then, draw a fence around each set of matching answers.

12)144	7)84	4)48	6)36	8)72
6)18	2)24	3)18	8)48	6)54
8)24	11)33	10)60	5)30	12)108
5)15	8)40	5)35	3)21	11)77
7)35	3)15	5)40	2)14	9)63
2)10	12)96	7)56	2)16	10)70

A. On the back of this paper, write four division problems that have the answers 2, 4, 10, and 11.

B. On another sheet of paper, write 20 division problems. Challenge a friend to solve the problems correctly in two minutes.

Make It Fair

Read each problem and draw a picture to show what is happening. Then, solve the problem.

1. Tony has 12 cookies. There are 6 children. How many cookies will each child get?

2. The pet shelter received a donation of 24 dog biscuits. Eight dogs are at the shelter. How many biscuits should each dog get?

3. Renee is making 5 pizzas. She has 25 pieces of pepperoni to divide between the pizzas. How many pieces of pepperoni should go on each pizza?

4. Mr. Ormand has 18 books to place on 3 shelves. He wants to put the same number of books on each shelf. How many books should he put on each shelf?

A. On the back of this paper, write four more division problems. Draw pictures to go with each problem.

B. On another sheet of paper, list at least 10 problems you would need to solve using division.

Hop to It!

Solve the division problems.

1. 5)65

2. 4)44

3. 8)96

4. 7)91

5. 3)54

6. 2)66

7. 6)78

8. 9)90

9. 3)45

10. 4)64

11. 5)95

12. 3)93

13. 2)84

14. 3)66

15. 6)84

16. 5)85

A. On the back of this paper, explain in words how to divide 74 by 2.

B. On another sheet of paper, make a list of times outside of school when it may be helpful to know how to divide.

Remainder Roundup

Solve the division problems. Use *r* to show the remainders.

1. 5)‾28‾

2. 7)‾45‾

3. 3)‾26‾

4. 8)‾26‾

5. 6)‾51‾

6. 9)‾65‾

7. 8)‾43‾

8. 9)‾59‾

9. 7)‾33‾

Try This!

A. On another sheet of paper, use multiplication and addition to check your answers.

B. On another sheet of paper, draw a picture to show what a remainder is.

CD-104538 • © Carson-Dellosa

Take a Spin

Turn the wheel and solve the division problems. Use *r* to show the remainders.

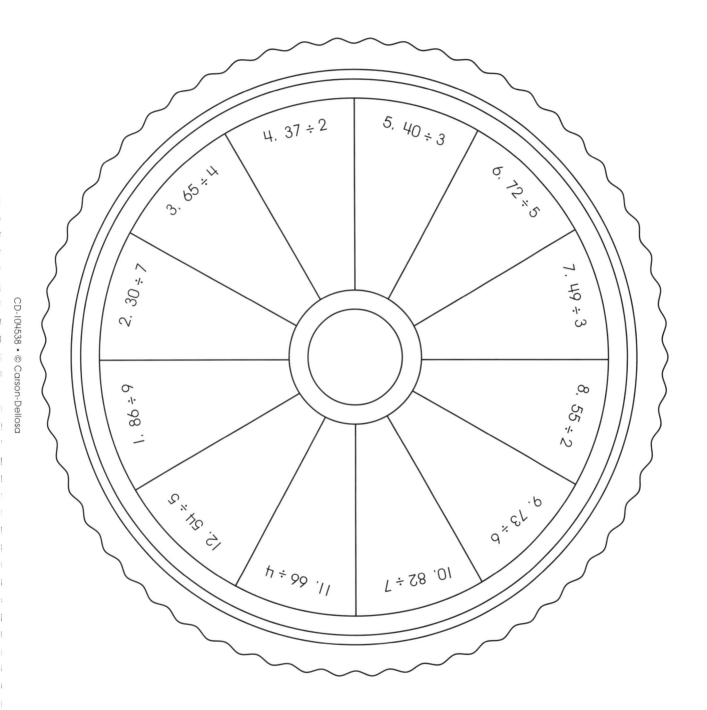

A. On the back of this paper, write and solve 10 additional division problems.

B. Use multiplication and addition to check your answers.

Cool!

To solve the riddle below, match the numbers with remainders and write the letters on the lines.

E. 5)‾3‾7‾   T. 3)‾2‾8‾   D. 5)‾1‾8‾   S. 6)‾4‾6‾

I. 4)‾3‾1‾   B. 3)‾3‾7‾   U. 8)‾4‾3‾   H. 10)‾3‾2‾

A. 12)‾7‾4‾   N. 4)‾2‾5‾   R. 8)‾8‾7‾   G. 6)‾1‾4‾

Why do teachers wear sunglasses?

___ ___ C ___ ___ ___ ___
12 r1 7 r2   6 r2 5 r3 7 r4 7 r2

___ ___ ___ ___ ___
9 r1 3 r2 7 r2 7 r3 10 r7

___ ___ ___ ___ ___ ___ ___ ___
7 r4 9 r1 5 r3 3 r3 7 r2 6 r1 9 r1 7 r4

___ ___ ___
6 r2 10 r7 7 r2

___ O
7 r4

___ R ___ ___ ___ ___ !
12 r1   7 r3 2 r2 3 r2 9 r1

Try This!

A. On another sheet of paper, make a poster that explains how to use reverse operations to check a division problem with remainders.

B. Write five more division problems that will have remainders. Challenge a friend to solve them correctly.

Popping Problems

Read each problem and write a number sentence to show what is happening. Then, solve the problem.

1. Stephen had 24 bags of popcorn to sell at the snack bar. He sold all of the popcorn to six customers. If each customer bought the same number of bags, how many bags did each customer buy?

2. Philip sold 69 buckets of popcorn. He worked for three weeks and sold the same amount each week. How many buckets of popcorn did he sell each week?

3. Brandon sold 88 buckets of popcorn in two weeks. If he sold the same amount each week, how many buckets of popcorn did he sell each week?

4. Kennedy popped 75 cups of popcorn in 3 days. If she popped the same number of cups each day, how many cups did she pop each day?

5. Ana popped 52 cups of popcorn in two days. Who popped more cups of popcorn, Kennedy or Ana?

6. Cody popped 76 cups of popcorn in four days. Did she pop more or fewer cups of popcorn than Kennedy and Ana?

 Try This!

A. Choose one of the problems above and draw a picture to show the problem and how you solved it.

B. On another sheet of paper, write three more word problems that need to be solved using division. Write a number sentence for each word problem.

Operation Options

Write the correct symbol in each oval. Use +, −, x, or ÷ .

1. 7 (×) 8 = 56

2. 54 ( ) 9 = 6

3. 36 ( ) 5 = 31

4. 12 ( ) 6 = 18

5. 72 ( ) 7 = 65

6. 18 ( ) 5 = 23

7. 40 ( ) 2 = 38

8. 8 ( ) 8 = 64

9. 62 ( ) 25 = 37

10. 48 ( ) 6 = 8

11. 32 ( ) 4 = 8

12. 6 ( ) 7 = 42

13. 72 ( ) 8 = 9

14. 45 ( ) 29 = 16

Try This!

A. On another sheet of paper, write a fact family for five problems above.

B. Write word problems to go along with the five problems above.

CD-104538 • © Carson-Dellosa

Testing 1, 2, 3

Solve the problems. Fill in the circle for the correct answer.

1. Brian solved two math problems.
   It took him 11 minutes to complete
   the first problem and 13 minutes to
   complete the second. How long did it
   take him to complete both problems?

   ○ A. 2 minutes
   ○ B. 24 minutes
   ○ C. 20 minutes
   ○ D. 24 hours

2. Mia invited 25 friends to her party.
   Only 17 friends showed up. How
   many friends did not come?

   ○ A. 42 friends
   ○ B. 12 friends
   ○ C. 9 friends
   ○ D. 8 friends

3. Shannon read 12 pages in her
   science book. She still has to read
   18 more pages. How many pages
   was she assigned to read?

   ○ A. 6 pages
   ○ B. 20 pages
   ○ C. 30 pages
   ○ D. 10 pages

4. Marcus reads 3 books each week.
   How many books will he finish in
   6 weeks?

   ○ A. 9 books
   ○ B. 3 books
   ○ C. 18 books
   ○ D. 21 books

5. Shelby is 3 inches taller than Kelsey.
   Kelsey is 4 feet 5 inches tall. How tall
   is Shelby?

   ○ A. 4 feet 3 inches
   ○ B. 4 feet 8 inches
   ○ C. 4 feet 2 inches
   ○ D. 4 feet 4 inches

6. Nikki baked 24 cookies. She wanted
   to give the same number of cookies
   to her 3 neighbors. How many
   cookies will she give each neighbor?

   ○ A. 8 cookies
   ○ B. 21 cookies
   ○ C. 6 cookies
   ○ D. 16 cookies

 Try This!

   A. On the back of this paper, write four word problems. Then, write the number sentence
   needed to solve each problem.

   B. On another sheet of paper, tell which problem you thought was the hardest to solve
   and why.

Money Bags

Read the value of the coins. Write the total on each money bag.

1. 1 quarter

   1 dime

   1 nickel

   2 pennies

2. 2 quarters

   1 dime

   1 nickel

   1 penny

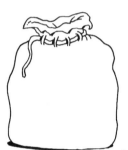

3. 3 quarters

   2 dimes

   2 pennies

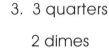

4. 1 quarter

   3 dimes

   2 nickels

   8 pennies

5. 2 quarters

   2 dimes

   3 nickels

   3 pennies

6. 1 quarter

   3 dimes

   4 nickels

   5 pennies

 **Try This!**

A. Number each money bag in order from the least amount to the greatest amount.

B. On the back of this paper, write as many different ways of combining coins to equal 15 cents.

It's Safe with Me Part 1

Draw or write the dollars and coins inside each safe.

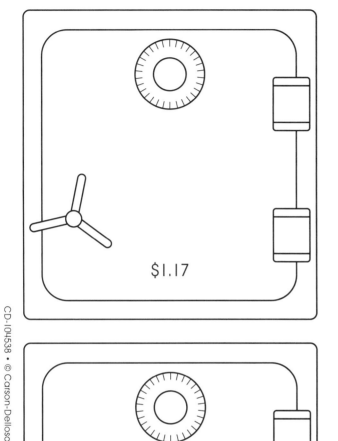

$1.17

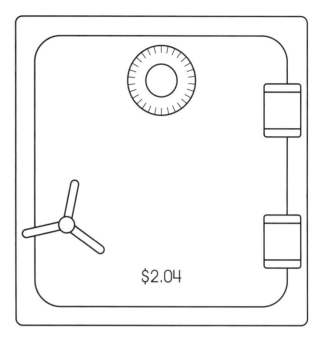

$2.04

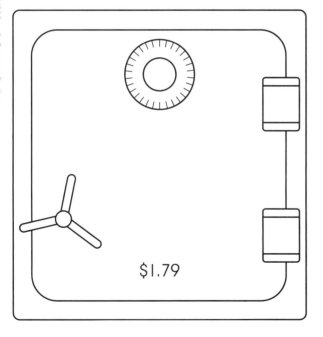

$1.79

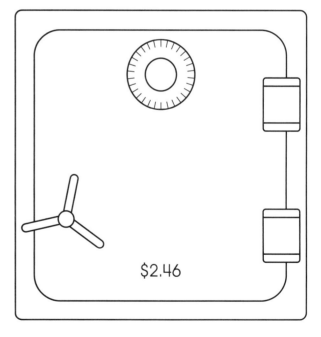

$2.46

A. The faces of previous presidents are shown on almost all U.S. currency. Why do you think this is?

B. Choose one of the amounts above and write 10 different combinations of dollars and coins that equal that amount.

It's Safe with Me Part 2

Draw or write the dollars and coins inside each safe.

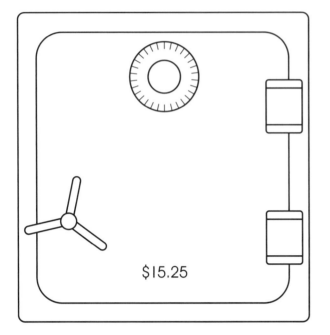

$15.25

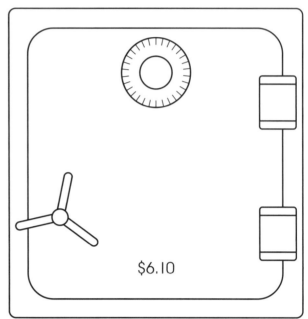

$6.10

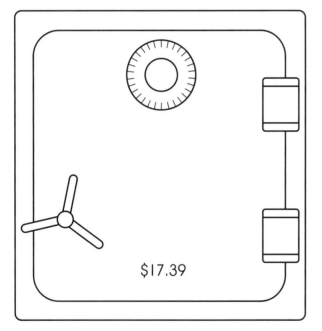

$17.39

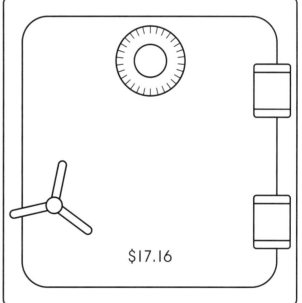

$17.16

Try This!

A. Order the value of the money in the safes from least to greatest.

B. Add the value of the four safes together. What is the total amount of money?

The Fewest Coins

Write the amount shown using the least number of coins to make that amount.

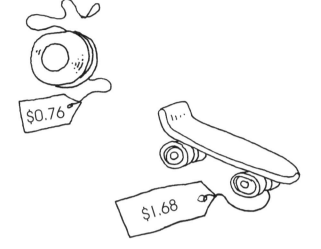

$0.76

$0.98

$1.68

$1.42

CD-104538 • © Carson-Dellosa

	Amount	Quarters	Dimes	Nickels	Pennies
1.	$0.76				
2.	$0.45				
3.	$0.98				
4.	$0.40				
5.	$0.84				
6.	$0.62				
7.	$1.42				
8.	$1.68				

Try This!

A. On another sheet of paper, make another chart like the one above. Then, figure out the most number of coins needed to make each amount.

B. Would you rather have the most number of coins possible or the least number of coins possible? Explain your answer on the back of this paper.

Name: _____

It Adds Up!

Add.

1. $42.13
   + 8.29

2. $14.56
   + 29.38

3. $22.65
   + 21.48

4. $19.31
   + 3.48

5. $46.73
   + 4.27

6. $61.49
   + 19.24

7. $33.42
   + 11.03

8. $50.84
   + 14.92

9. $27.49
   + 38.21

Try This!

A. Write in words how you would add $4.26 and $16.12. Then add.

B. Imagine that you found a receipt that has the amounts $15.95, $2.50, $12.00, and $7.25. Write what you would have bought with each amount and then add to find the total amount spent.

Spending Spree

Write the prices for each item. Then, add to find the total cost of the two items.

1.

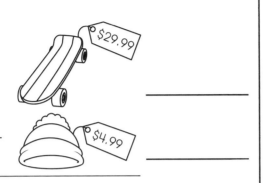

$29.99

+ $4.99

_____

_____

2.

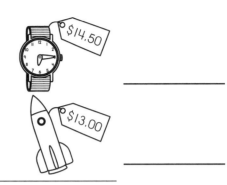

$14.50

+ $13.00

_____

_____

3.

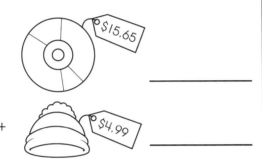

$15.65

+ $4.99

_____

_____

4.

$14.50

$25.50

_____

+

_____

5.

$13.00

+ $8.99

_____

_____

6.

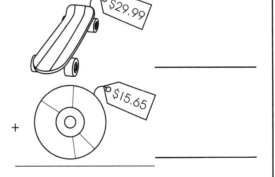

$29.99

$15.65

_____

+

_____

Try This!

A. Which two items would you most like to buy? How much would the two items cost?

B. Imagine that you have $50.00 to spend. On another sheet of paper, write about how you would spend it on these items and how much money you would have left.

You Had, You Spent

Read and solve the problems.

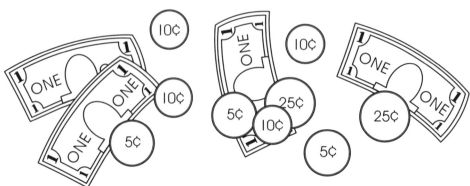

1. You had $23.45.

    You spent $3.95.

    You have _____ left.

2. You had $14.84.

    You spent $12.45.

    You have _____ left.

3. You had $40.29.

    You spent $31.13.

    You have _____ left.

4. You had $26.42.

    You spent $13.45.

    You have _____ left.

5. You had $61.49.

    You spent $47.29.

    You have _____ left.

6. You had $16.80.

    You spent $9.31.

    You have _____ left.

A. On another sheet of paper, write about something you want to buy. Tell how much it costs and how much money you have saved up. Tell how much money you still need to save or how much money you will have left.

B. Choose one of the problems above. On another sheet of paper, write a story that tells about the money you had, how you spent it, and how much you have left.

CD-104538 • © Carson-Dellosa

Order Up! Part 1

Read the menu. Then, answer the questions.

Menu			
Chicken Nuggets	$1.95		
PB&J Sandwich	$2.50	Milk	$1.25
Hamburger	$3.25	Water	$1.25
(with cheese add $0.75)		Soft Drink	$2.00
Chicken Sandwich	$4.15	Juice	$2.25
Soup	$2.25	Ice Cream	$3.75
Salad	$2.25	Yogurt	$2.00
Fruit	$1.75	Pie	$3.25
Chips	$2.00	Milkshake	$2.25
Fries	$3.25		

1. What would you order at this restaurant? _____

2. What is the total cost of your order? _____

A. If you had $5.00 to spend at this restaurant, what would you buy, and how much would you have left?

B. On the back of this paper, write an order to feed everyone in your family. Then, add to find the total cost of the meal.

Order Up! Part 2

Read each order. Then, use the menu on page 217 to figure out how much each meal cost.

1.

chicken nuggets

salad

milk

2.

fruit

yogurt

water

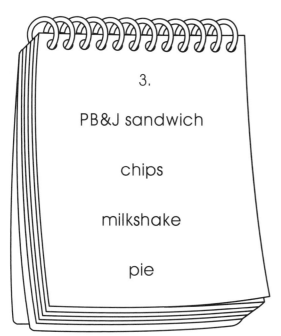

3.

PB&J sandwich

chips

milkshake

pie

4.

hamburger with cheese

fruit

soft drink

Try This!

A. How much change would you get back from each order above if you had $10.00 to start with? Solve the problems on the back of this paper.

B. How much change would you get back from each order above if you had $15.75 to start with? Solve the problems on the back of this paper.

Big Discount

Read the flyer. Then, figure out the new sale price of each item.

HUGE TOY SALE!

Original Price	Discount
$3.00–5.00	$1.00
$6.00–10.00	$2.00
$11.00–15.00	$3.00
$16.00–20.00	$4.00
$21.00–25.00	$5.00

$3.00	$12.00	$25.00
$8.00	$6.00	$5.00
$24.00	$22.00	$15.00

 **Try This!**

A. Choose two toys. Figure out how much the two toys would cost altogether at the discounted price.

B. If you were to buy all of the toys, how much would they cost in all at regular price? How much would they cost in all with the discount? Show your work on the back of this paper.

Money Problems?

Solve the money problems.

1. Mariah receives an allowance of $2.25 a week. This week, her mom paid her in nickels, dimes, and quarters. She received more dimes than quarters. What coins did her mom use to pay her?

2. Christopher wants to buy a remote control dinosaur that costs $56.50. He has saved $38.75. His uncle gave him $10.00 for helping clean his yard. How much more money does Christopher need?

3. Mr. Wagner takes his family on a trip to the amusement park. The tickets to get into the amusement park are $8.75 for adults and $5.75 for children. How much money will Mr. Wagner spend to buy tickets for himself, Mrs. Wagner, and their 2 children?

4. Carlos saved spare coins in a jar. When the jar was full, he counted the coins. He had 45 quarters, 65 dimes, 75 nickels, and 129 pennies. How much did Carlos have in all?

CD-104538 • © Carson-Dellosa

Try This!

A. On the back of this paper, draw a picture to show how you solved one of the problems above.

B. Write a letter to one of the people in the problems above to explain how to solve his or her money problems.

Name: _____

Parts of a Whole

Color to show the fractions.

1. $\frac{2}{3}$

2. $\frac{1}{5}$

3. $\frac{4}{6}$

4. $\frac{1}{2}$

5. $\frac{1}{4}$

6. $\frac{3}{3}$

7. $\frac{3}{5}$

8. $\frac{3}{4}$

9. $\frac{5}{6}$

A. On the back of this paper, write a fraction for each of the parts not colored in the rectangles above.

B. On the back of this paper, draw another shape to illustrate each fraction above.

Pizza Parlor

Draw a line to match the amount of each pizza to its fraction.

1.

A. $\dfrac{5}{6}$

2.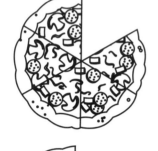

B. $\dfrac{5}{8}$

3.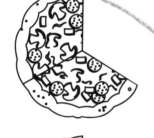

C. $\dfrac{1}{4}$

4.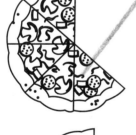

D. $\dfrac{2}{3}$

5.

E. $\dfrac{1}{2}$

 Try This!

A. On the back of this paper, draw a pizza that has $\dfrac{2}{8}$ pepperoni and $\dfrac{6}{8}$ cheese toppings.

B. On another sheet of paper, draw the following pizzas: 1 $\dfrac{1}{2}$ pepperoni pizzas, $\dfrac{1}{2}$ meat lover's pizza, 1 $\dfrac{1}{3}$ vegetarian pizzas, and $\dfrac{2}{3}$ cheese pizza.

Cheesy!

Color the fraction on the cheese. Then, cut out the cards. Glue each mouse to the top of a sheet of paper. Glue each equivalent fraction below the correct mouse.

Try This!

A. Under each column on your paper, draw another fraction that is equivalent.

B. On another sheet of paper, write 10 different fractions equivalent to $\frac{1}{2}$. What pattern do you see?

Which Is More?

Color the fractions and then compare. Use >, <, or = to make each number sentence true.

1.

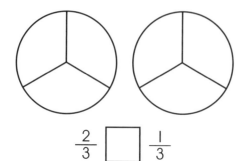

$\frac{2}{3}$ ☐ $\frac{1}{3}$

2.

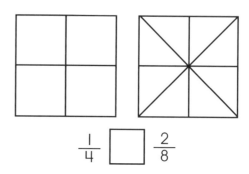

$\frac{1}{4}$ ☐ $\frac{2}{8}$

3.

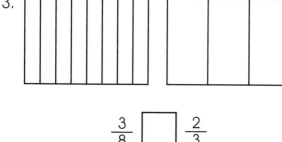

$\frac{3}{8}$ ☐ $\frac{2}{3}$

4.

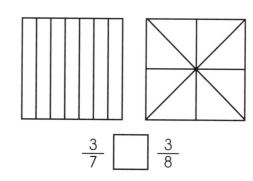

$\frac{3}{7}$ ☐ $\frac{3}{8}$

5.

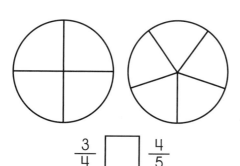

$\frac{3}{4}$ ☐ $\frac{4}{5}$

6.

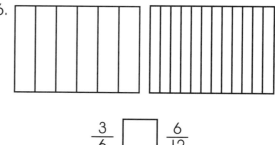

$\frac{3}{6}$ ☐ $\frac{6}{12}$

A. On another sheet of paper, draw a Venn diagram. Label one circle "More Than $\frac{1}{2}$" and the other circle "Less Than $\frac{1}{2}$." Place the following fractions in the diagram: $\frac{3}{6}$, $\frac{5}{8}$, $\frac{7}{9}$, $\frac{2}{4}$, $\frac{6}{7}$, $\frac{4}{8}$, $\frac{3}{4}$, $\frac{1}{3}$, $\frac{2}{5}$.

B. On the back of this paper, explain in words how to compare two fractions.

Name: _____

Fraction Strips

Study the fraction strips. Then, answer the questions.

1							
$\frac{1}{2}$				$\frac{1}{2}$			
$\frac{1}{3}$		$\frac{1}{3}$			$\frac{1}{3}$		
$\frac{1}{4}$		$\frac{1}{4}$		$\frac{1}{4}$		$\frac{1}{4}$	
$\frac{1}{5}$	$\frac{1}{5}$		$\frac{1}{5}$		$\frac{1}{5}$		$\frac{1}{5}$
$\frac{1}{6}$	$\frac{1}{6}$	$\frac{1}{6}$	$\frac{1}{6}$		$\frac{1}{6}$		$\frac{1}{6}$
$\frac{1}{8}$	$\frac{1}{8}$	$\frac{1}{8}$	$\frac{1}{8}$	$\frac{1}{8}$	$\frac{1}{8}$	$\frac{1}{8}$	$\frac{1}{8}$

1. Write fractions equal to 1. _____

2. Write fractions equal to $\frac{1}{2}$. _____

3. Write fractions equal to $\frac{1}{4}$. _____

Try This!

A. Show what a fraction strip would look like divided into seven parts.

B. One the back of this paper, copy the fraction strips. Then, add strips that include sevenths, ninths, tenths, elevenths, and twelfths.

Know-It-All

Use >, <, or = to make each number sentence true.

1. $\dfrac{1}{2}$ [<] $\dfrac{2}{3}$

2. $\dfrac{1}{6}$ [ ] $\dfrac{2}{8}$

3. $\dfrac{1}{5}$ [<] $\dfrac{1}{8}$

4. $\dfrac{5}{6}$ [ ] $\dfrac{4}{8}$

5. $\dfrac{2}{2}$ [<] $\dfrac{2}{4}$

6. $\dfrac{4}{8}$ [ ] $\dfrac{3}{6}$

7. $\dfrac{4}{4}$ [<] $\dfrac{3}{10}$

8. $\dfrac{10}{12}$ [ ] $\dfrac{4}{5}$

9. $\dfrac{3}{5}$ [>] $\dfrac{6}{8}$

10. $\dfrac{7}{10}$ [ ] $\dfrac{11}{12}$

A. On another sheet of paper, draw pictures of five of the comparisons above.

B. On the back of this paper, write the fractions above in order from smallest to largest.

Name: _____

You Rule!

Estimate the measurement of each item below. Then, use a ruler to measure the items. Write the measurements to the nearest inch.

	Estimated Measurement	Actual Measurement
pencil		
tissue box		
door		
scissors		
paper clip		
keyboard		
calculator		

Try This!

A. Measure each item again using centimeters. Record your answers on the back of this paper.

B. On the back of this paper, write the items in order from smallest to largest.

Name: _____

Measure the Line

Use yarn or string to cover each line. Then, use a ruler to measure the length of yarn or string. Write the measurements in inches.

1. _____ inches

2. _____ inches

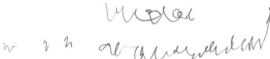

3. _____ inches

4. _____ inches

5. _____ inches

Try This!

A. On the back of this paper, draw five other lines. Measure the lines to the nearest inch.

B. Now, measure each line on this page to the nearest centimeter. Write the measurements.

Name: _____

Inchworms?

Measure the worms. Write the length of each worm to the closest $\frac{1}{2}$ inch and centimeter. Use a string to help you measure.

1.

_____ inches

_____ centimeters

2.

_____ inches

_____ centimeters

3.

_____ inches

_____ centimeters

4.

_____ inches

_____ centimeters

5.

_____ inches

_____ centimeters

6.

_____ inches

_____centimeters

A. On another sheet of paper, draw five more worms and measure each one. Write the measurements in inches and centimeters.

B. On the back of this paper, write a paragraph that compares inches to centimeters.

Measurement Matters

Read the conversions. Then, solve the problems.

> 1 foot = 12 inches
>
> 1 yard = 3 feet or 36 inches

1. 12 yards   = _____ feet

2. 5 feet   = _____ inches

3. 24 inches   = _____ feet

4. 2 yards   = _____ inches

5. 6 yards   = _____ inches

6. 12 feet   = _____ yards

7. 4 feet   = _____ inches

8. 21 yards   = _____ feet

9. 39 inches   = _____ feet and _____ inches

10. 15 yards   = _____ feet or _____ inches

A. On the back of this paper, write three things you would measure in inches, three things you would measure in feet, and three things you would measure in yards.

B. Make a poster that lists the measurement equivalents for inches, yards, feet, millimeters, centimeters, kilometers, and meters.

CD-104538 • © Carson-Dellosa

Name: _____   Measuring Liquids

In the Kitchen

Read the conversions. Then, solve the problems.

> 1 pint = 2 cups
> 1 quart = 2 pints or 4 cups
> 1 gallon = 4 quarts, 8 pints, or 16 cups

1. 2 pints   = _____ cups

2. 2 gallons = _____ quarts

3. 4 quarts = _____ cups

4. 4 gallons = _____ pints

5. 3 pints   = _____ cups

6. 3 quarts = _____ cups

7. 32 cups = _____ gallons

8. 64 cups = _____ quarts

9. How many gallons of ice cream would you need to feed 64 people $\frac{1}{2}$-cup servings? _____

10. How many pints of milk would you need for a recipe that calls for 16 cups of milk? _____

A. Make a poster that illustrates liquid measurement equivalents. Use pictures, not words.

B. On the back of this paper, draw two items that could be measured in each unit: cup, pint, quart, and gallon.

CD-104538 • © Carson-Dellosa

Lunchtime

Circle the correct unit of measure.

1. bowl of soup

   c.   gal.

2. carton of milk

   L   mL

3. bottle of water

   gal.   L

4. jug of juice

   mL   gal.

5. juice box

   c.   qt.

6. pot of water

   mL   qt.

Estimate how many units it will take to fill each item.

7. pitcher

_____ cartons of milk

8. large pot

_____ bottles of water

9. sink

_____ jugs of juice

A. On the back of this paper, list five items from around your school that contain liquid. Write the amount of liquid in each.

B. On another sheet of paper, make a poster that lists the customary and metric units of measure.

Measure Up

Under each picture, write the unit of measurement (ounces, pounds, or tons) that the object would be measured in.

16 ounces = a pound
2,000 pounds = a ton

1.  _____	2.  _____	3.  _____
4.  _____	5.  _____	6.  _____
7.  _____	8.  _____	9.  _____

Try This!

A. On another sheet of paper, for each unit of measurement (ounces, pounds, and tons), draw a picture of an object measured in that unit.

B. On another sheet of paper, make a poster that gives the definition of measurements (ounce, pounds, and tons) and examples of each.

Experiment a Little!

Read the conversions. Then, draw a line to match each weight with its equivalent.

16 ounces = 1 pound
2,000 pounds = 1 ton
1,000 grams = 1 kilogram

1. 16 ounces

2. 4,000 pounds

3. 3 kilograms

4. 1 ton

5. 80,000 ounces

6. 10,000 grams

7. 8 pounds

8. $\frac{1}{2}$ kilogram

A. 3,000 grams

B. 1 pound

C. 5,000 pounds

D. 128 ounces

E. 500 grams

F. 10 kilograms

G. 32,000 ounces

H. 2 tons

A. How much does a 10-pound bag of potatoes weigh in ounces?

B. Write a letter to your senator to explain why you think the United States should switch to measuring mass in grams and kilograms.

CD-104538 • © Carson-Dellosa

Bubbles, Bubbles

Solve the problems. Color the correct answers. Cross out the incorrect answers.

1. Alex blew bubbles in his driveway. The bubble that traveled the farthest flew 5 feet. How many inches did it travel?

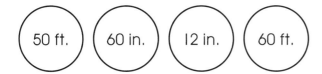

(50 ft.) (60 in.) (12 in.) (60 ft.)

2. Alex got a gallon of bubbles for his birthday. How many quarts did he have?

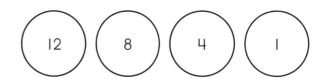

(12) (8) (4) (1)

3. If Alex blows bubbles 3 feet into the air and then the wind blows them 24 inches higher, how high did the bubbles blow in all?

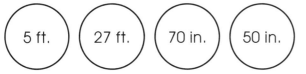

(5 ft.) (27 ft.) (70 in.) (50 in.)

4. Alex had one gallon of bubbles. He thinks that if he pours out two quarts of bubbles, he will have four pints left. Is he right?

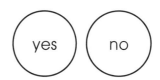

(yes) (no)

A. On the back of this paper, write your own measurement problem about Alex and his bubbles. Then, solve the problem.

B. On another sheet of paper, write a letter to your teacher to explain why it is or is not important to know how to convert measurements.

It's Getting Hot!

Read the thermometer. *F* stands for Fahrenheit. *C* stands for Celsius. Answer the questions.

1. At what temperature does water boil?

   _____°F   _____°C

2. At what temperature does water freeze?

   _____°F   _____°C

3. If the temperature outside is 92°F, would

   you wear a coat? _____

4. Could it snow if the temperature is 29°F?

   _____

5. If the temperature outside is 4°C, would

   you wear a coat? _____

6. If the temperature outside is 36°F,

   would you most likely ice skate or swim?

   _____

7. Circle the temperature that would be

   best for a picnic.   20°F   78°F   90°C

8. Circle the temperature that would be

   best for building a snowman.

   0°C   60°F   75°C

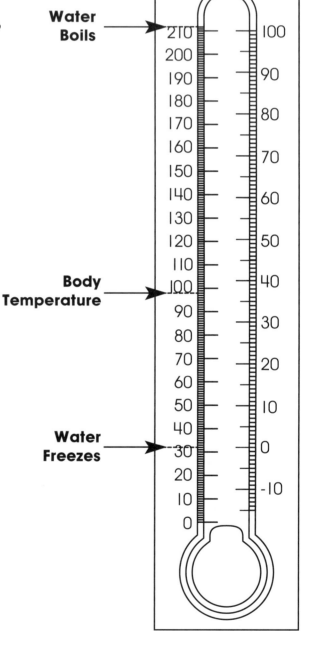

CD-104538 • © Carson-Dellosa

A. On the back of this paper, write five more questions about temperature. Have a friend answer the questions.

B. On the back of this paper, explain the difference between Celsius and Fahrenheit.

Today's Weather

Label each thermometer to match the temperature given.

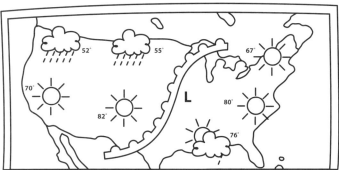

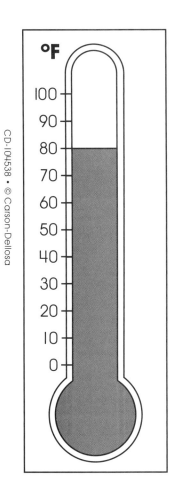

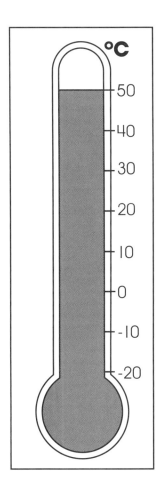

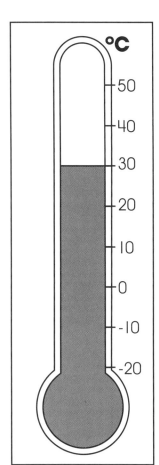

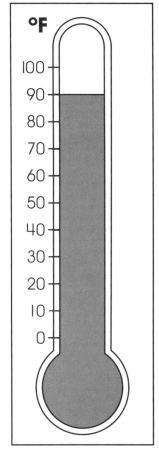

_____   _____   _____   _____

A. On the back of this paper, write a story that involves weather and reading a thermometer.

B. On another sheet of paper, draw and label your own thermometer. Be sure to include both Celsius and Fahrenheit.

Got the Time?

Write the time on each clock.

1.

7:00

2.

1:30

3.

2:00

4.

10:00

5.

4:30

6.

1:30

7.

3:15

8.

2:45

9.

9:15

Try This!

A. On the back of this paper, write the times that school starts and ends. Then, draw each time on a clock.

B. Think about your daily schedule. On another sheet of paper, write the times of six events. Then, draw a clock to show each time.

CD-104538 • © Carson-Dellosa

Time's Up! Part 1

Cut out the cards. Then, match the cards that show the same time. Make up a game to play with a friend. Use the cards on page 240 for your game too.

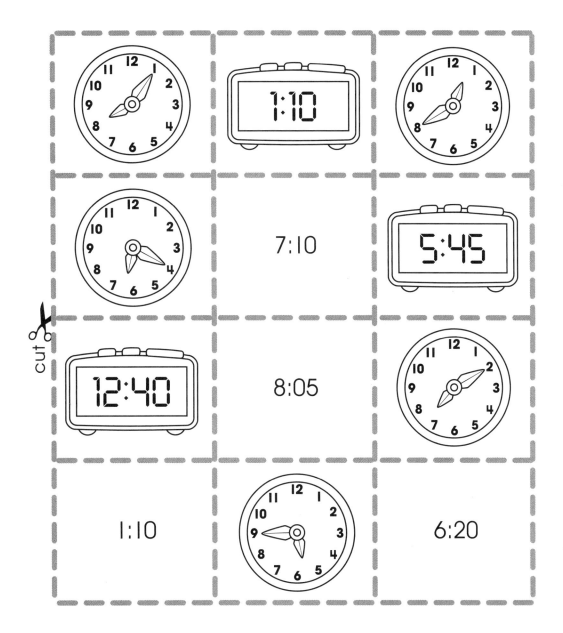

CD-104538 • © Carson-Dellosa

Try This!

A. Look at a clock in your classroom and write the time on another sheet of paper. Write the time three different ways.

B. Make a poster that explains different time vocabulary including *quarter after*, *quarter to*, *half past*, *minute hand*, and *hour hand*.

Time's Up! Part 2

Cut out the cards. Then, match the cards that show the same time. Make up a game to play with a friend. Use the cards on page 239 for your game too.

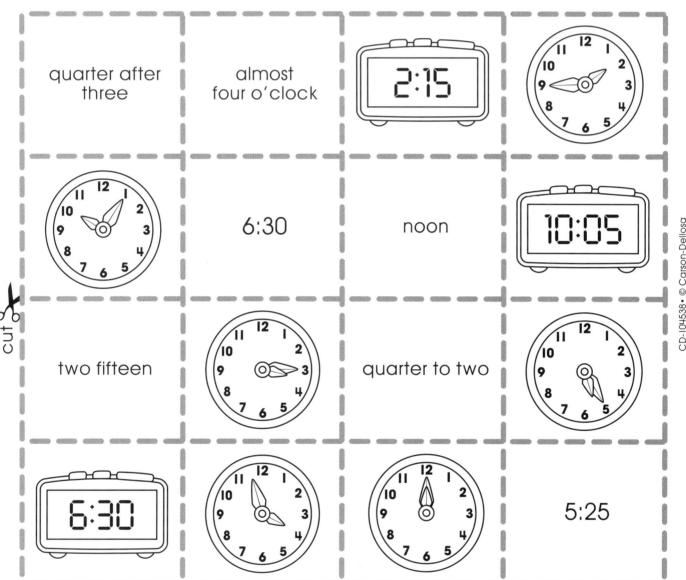

CD-104538 • © Carson-Dellosa

Try This!

A. On another sheet of paper, write the times that you wake up and go to bed. Write the times in three different ways.

B. On another sheet of paper, write something that you do each hour during the day. Write the times that you do each thing.

Name: _____

Ticktock

Draw hands on each clock to match the time.

1.

3:35

2.

10:05

3.

4:55

4.

8:10

5.

12:50

6.

9:20

7.

7:25

8.
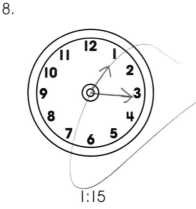

1:15

9.

11:40

Try This!

A. Imagine that a friend has missed the math lesson on telling time. On another sheet of paper, write how you would explain telling time to your friend.

B. Sixty seconds are in one minute. Sixty minutes are in one hour. Twenty-four hours are in one day. How many seconds are in one day? Use another sheet of paper to find the answer.

All Hands on Deck

Read and solve the problems.

1. Brooke woke up at 6:05 A.M. She had 55 minutes to report for duty. What time did Brooke need to arrive for duty?

2. Brooke's shift started at 7:00 A.M. She was scheduled to work $5\frac{1}{2}$ hours. What time would her shift be over?

3. Brooke arrived at the gym to work out at 1:15 P.M. Her workout took 45 minutes. What time was Brooke done at the gym?

4. Brooke met friends for dinner at 7:00 P.M. She spent 3 hours and 20 minutes with her friends. What time did she leave her friends?

5. Brooke called her sister at 8:10 P.M. They talked for 47 minutes. What time did Brooke get off the phone?

6. Brooke went to bed at 10:00 P.M. She woke up the next morning at 6:00 A.M. How many hours did she sleep?

Try This!

A. How many times a day does the hour hand move across the number 12 on the face of a clock? Explain your answer on another sheet of paper.

B. On another sheet of paper, write six time problems about your day. Have a friend solve the problems.

Take Your Time

Write the time shown on each clock. Then, find the time elapsed between each pair of times.

1.

_____   _____

Elapsed Time: _____

2.

_____   _____

Elapsed Time: _____

3.

_____   _____

Elapsed Time: _____

4.

_____   _____

Elapsed Time: _____

5.

_____   _____

Elapsed Time: _____

6.

_____   _____

Elapsed Time: _____

Try This!

A. Think of an activity you do. Write the time you start the activity and the time the activity ends. How much time does the activity take?

B. On another sheet of paper, write your daily school schedule. Figure out how much time elapses between each event.

It's Time!

Solve the problems.

1.

Nathan is supposed to be at school in 10 minutes. What time should he get there?

2.

Nathan started breakfast at 7:10 A.M. It took him 15 minutes to eat. What time did he finish eating?

3.

Nathan will leave school in 5 minutes. What time will he leave?

4.

Nathan will go to the park in 15 minutes. What time will he go to the park?

5.

Nathan will eat dinner in 15 minutes. What time will he eat?

6.

Nathan will start his homework in five minutes. What time will he start his homework?

A. On the back of this paper, write the time you arrive at school and the time you leave to go home. How much time do you spend at school each day?

B. On another sheet of paper, write your weekend schedule. Then, figure out how much time you spend on each event.

Dive In!

Find the area of each shape. (Each square equals 1.)

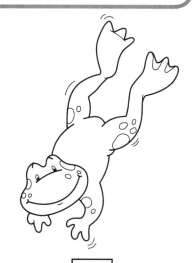

1.

5

2

Area = 10

2.

Area = _____

3.

4

Area = _____

4.

Area = _____

5.

Area = _____

6.

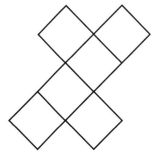

Area = _____

A. On a sheet of grid paper, draw four more shapes and find the area of each shape.

B. Draw a square with the area of one. Then, draw a square with the area of four. What is the next size square?

Name: _____

Draw It!

Draw a shape to match the area.

1.

Area = 10 square units

2.

Area = 8 square units

3.

Area = 5 square units

4.

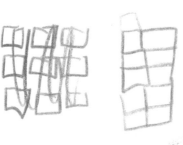

Area = 11 square units

5.

Area = 12 square units

6.

Area = 9 square units

Try This!

A. On a sheet of grid paper, draw a swimming pool. Then, find the area of your pool.

B. Imagine that smaller squares were used to form all of the shapes on this page. Would your answers change, or would they stay the same? Explain your answer on the back of this paper.

Name: _____

Fenced In

Find the perimeter of each shape.

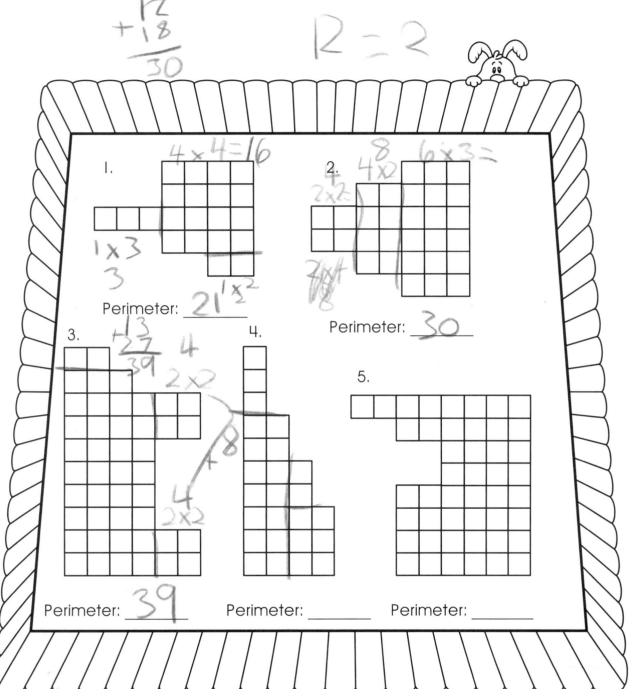

1.

Perimeter: 21

2.

Perimeter: 30

3.

Perimeter: 39

4.

Perimeter: _____

5.

Perimeter: _____

 **Try This!**

A. On a sheet of grid paper, draw three more shapes. Find the perimeter of each shape.

B. On another sheet of paper, explain the difference between area and perimeter.

Down the Middle

Draw each matching part to make the object symmetrical.

1.

2.

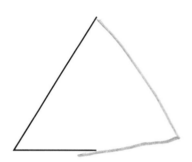

3.

4.

5.

6.

Try This!

A. On the back of this paper, draw three more pictures that show symmetry.

B. On another sheet of paper, draw a square and a rectangle. Draw all possible lines of symmetry in each shape.

How Many Lines?

Draw each line of symmetry on the objects. Then, write the number of lines of symmetry in the circle.

1. 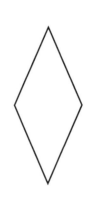 ◯

2. 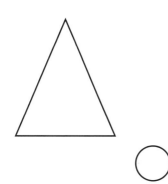 ◯

3.  ◯

4. 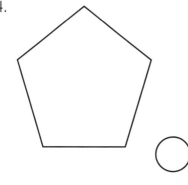 ◯

5. 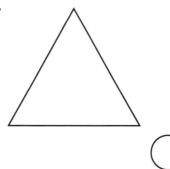 ◯

6. 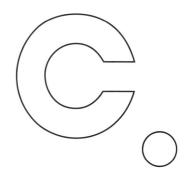 ◯

7. 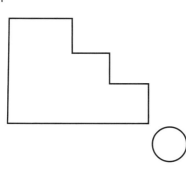 ◯

8. 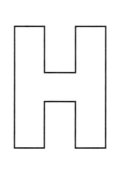 ◯

9. 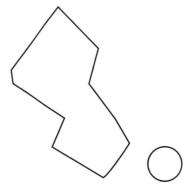 ◯

A. Draw two more new shapes with two lines of symmetry.

B. On another sheet of paper, list at least 10 situations in which knowing symmetry would be helpful.

Shape Up!

Complete the information for each polygon.

1.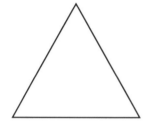

Number of sides: _____

Name: _____

2.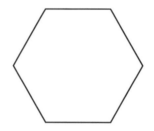

Number of sides: _____

Name: _____

3.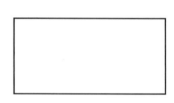

Number of sides: _____

Name: _____

4.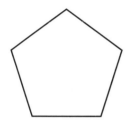

Number of sides: _____

Name: _____

5.

Number of sides: _____

Name: _____

6.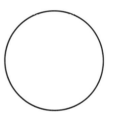

Number of sides: _____

Name: _____

7.

Number of sides: _____

Name: _____

8.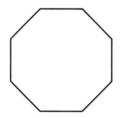

Number of sides: _____

Name: _____

9.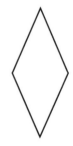

Number of sides: _____

Name: _____

Try This!

A. Divide another sheet of paper in half. On one side, draw three polygons and write the definition of a polygon. On the other side, draw three non-polygons and explain why they are not polygons.

B. Make a poster that illustrates six different polygons and the attributes of each. For example: A square has four sides of equal length and four right angles.

Draw-a-gon

Draw three examples of each polygon.

quadrilaterals	rhombuses
squares	rectangles
parallelograms	trapezoids

CD-104538 • © Carson-Dellosa

Try This!

A. On another sheet of paper, draw a picture using as many polygons as possible. Label each polygon.

B. On another sheet of paper, explain why not all quadrilaterals are parallelograms, but why all parallelograms are quadrilaterals.

On the Hunt

Find at least three examples of each polygon around your classroom, home, or school. Write the name of each object in the correct section.

Triangle	Square
	Pentagon
Rectangle	
	Hexagon

Try This!

A. A decagon has 10 sides. On the back of this paper, draw a decagon.

B. On another sheet of paper, write a poem or a song to help you remember the names of polygons.

Right, Acute, or Obtuse?

Write *right*, *acute*, or *obtuse* to describe each angle.

1.

_____

2.

_____

3.

_____

4.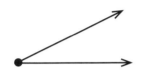

_____

5.

_____

6.

_____

Trace the angle in each picture with a color.

7.

right angle

8.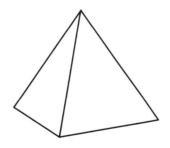

obtuse angle

9.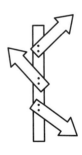

acute angle

Try This!

A. Find examples of right, acute, and obtuse angles in your classroom. List them on the back of this paper.

B. Draw a picture of a robot using as many angles as possible. Trace all acute angles with red, all obtuse angles with blue, and all right angles with green.

Triangle Mysteries

Unscramble the letters to label each type of triangle.

1.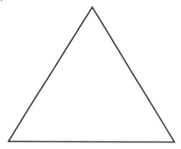

_____
(ieueaalrltq)

2.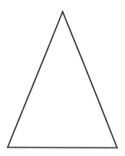

_____
(eeoiscssl)

3.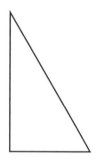

_____
(itrhg)

Draw a picture to match each description. Then, label each triangle.

4. Draw a triangle with one right angle.

5. Draw a triangle with all sides the same length.

6. Draw a triangle with only two sides the same length.

_____   _____   _____

CD-104538 • © Carson-Dellosa

Try This!

A. On the back of this paper, describe the types of angles found in each type of triangle.

B. On another sheet of paper, draw a picture of your favorite place to spend your free time. Use as many triangles as possible.

Flip, Slide, and Turn

Compare each pair of pictures. Tell how each picture changed by writing *flip*, *slide*, or *turn*.

1.

_____

2.

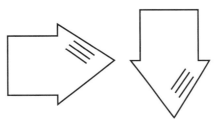

_____

3.

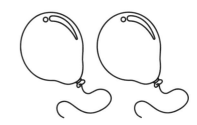

_____

4.

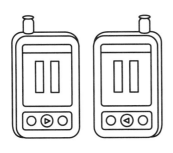

_____

5.

_____

6.

_____

7.

_____

8.

_____

9.

_____

A. On the back of this paper, draw a smiley face. Then, draw it flipped, slid, and turned.

B. On another sheet of paper, write *flip*, *slide*, and *turn* on the left side of the paper. Write *translation*, *rotation*, and *reflection* down the right side. Draw a line to match each term to its meaning.

Wake-Up Routine

Compare each pair of pictures. Write if the picture shows a flip, a slide, or a turn.

  _____

 _____

 _____

Try This!

A. Draw a picture of an object in your classroom. Then, draw a picture that shows a flip, a slide, or a turn.

B. Trace a picture from one of your favorite books onto a sheet of paper. Then, draw its flip, slide, and turn.

Solid Work

Write the name of each solid. Circle each vertex. Color each edge blue and each face yellow.

1.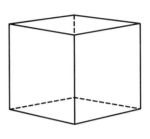

_____

2.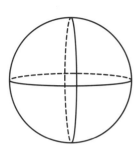

_____

3.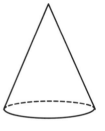

_____

4.

_____

5.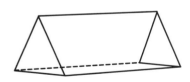

_____

6.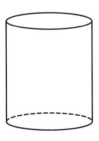

_____

Try This!

A. Find examples of four geometric solids in your classroom or home. Draw them on another sheet of paper.

B. Make a poster that includes six geometric solids. Tell how many faces, vertices, and edges each solid has.

If the Jacket Fits

Draw a line to match each solid with its jacket.

1.

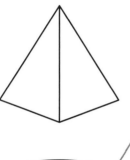

2.

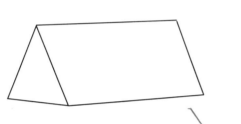

3.

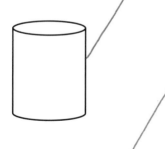

4.

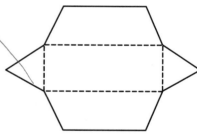

5.

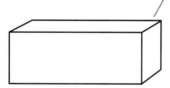

A.

B.

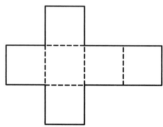

C.

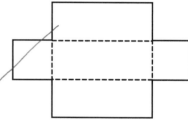

D.

E.

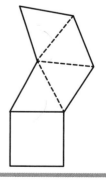

 Try This!

A. Write a riddle for one of the solids above. Be sure to give hints about its faces.

B. Use a sheet of grid paper to make a jacket for a cube. Then, fold and tape the jacket to make a cube.

Figure It Out

Read each riddle. Then, write the name of the solid described and draw a picture of it.

1. I have six faces all exactly the same. You might roll me in a game. I am a _____.	2. I have six faces. Each face has an exact match. Some cereal comes in a shape like me. I am a _____.
3. I have one rectangular face and two circle faces. I'm the same shape as a soft drink can. I am a _____.	4. I have a square face and four triangle faces. You can see me in Egypt. I am a _____.

 **Try This!**

A. Write your own riddles for each solid. Then, have a friend try to solve the riddles.

B. On another sheet of paper, draw a picture made entirely out of solids. Try to use at least one of each of the solids shown above. Label each solid in your picture.

Beautiful Backyards

Solve the problems. Draw pictures to help you.

1. Monique is going to mow her backyard. Each side of her yard is 10 feet long. The total distance around the yard is 50 feet. What shape is her yard?

2. The flower bed in Monique's yard is rectangular. If one side is 3 feet long, draw a picture of what the flower bed looks like.

3. Monique raked the leaves in her yard. She put all of them in a trash can with a round lid. What shape was the trash can?

4. Monique took a break from yard work to swing on her swing set. What type of lines do the chains on her swing probably make?

Try This!

A. On another sheet of paper, draw an imaginary backyard using as many geometric shapes as possible.

B. On the back of this paper, make a chart that gives tips on how to remember the names of geometric shapes and what they mean.

Picturing Pets Part 1

Noah collected data about his classmates' favorite pets. Color the graph to show the data he collected. Then, use the information on the graph to answer the questions on page 262.

Favorite Pets

cats	6
dogs	6
gerbils	4
goldfish	3
iguanas	1

Favorite Pets

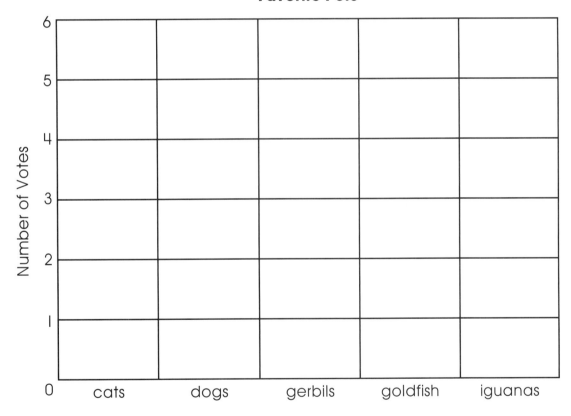

A. Collect data about your classmates' favorite pets. Draw a graph to show the information.

B. On another sheet of paper, explain why a graph is a good way to show data collected. Include other types of information that could be shown on a graph.

Picturing Pets Part 2

Read the graph on page 261 and answer the questions.

1. What information does the graph show? _____

2. How many children voted for gerbils? _____

3. What pet received the fewest votes? _____

4. Which two pets received an equal number of votes? _____

5. How many votes did goldfish and gerbils receive altogether?
_____

6. How many more children voted for cats than goldfish? _____

7. How many children voted in all? _____

8. What information does this graph *not* show? _____

A. Draw pictures to add your own vote and the votes of three of your friends to the graph.

B. On the back of this paper, draw a new graph to show the information using numbers instead of pictures.

Flower Power Part 1

Madeline made a list of the flowers she planted in her garden. Record the information on her list on both graphs. Then, answer the questions on page 264.

Flowers in My Garden

daisies	8
roses	5
sunflowers	2
tulips	6

Picture Graph

 Daisies	
 Roses	
 Sunflowers	
 Tulips	

Bar Graph

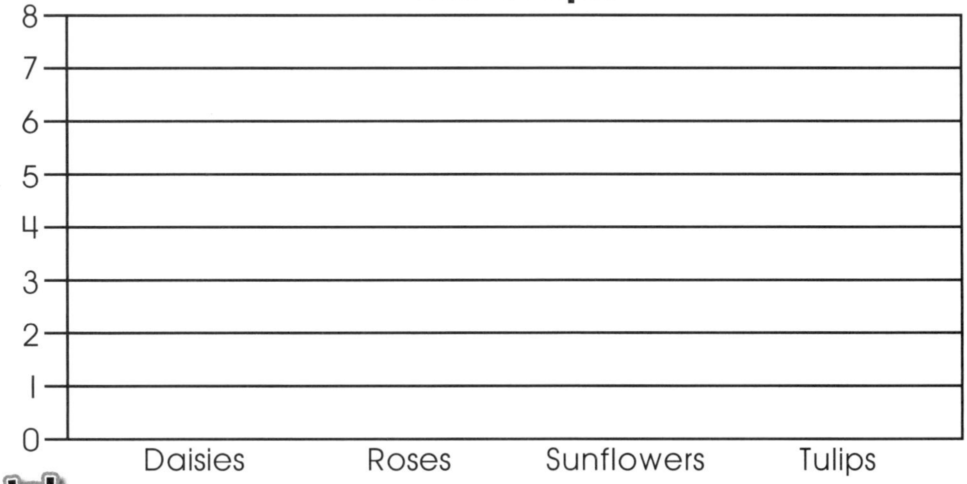

Try This!

A. Which graph do you prefer? Explain your reasons.

B. Ask your classmates about their favorite foods. Then, draw a graph to show the information on another sheet of paper.

Flower Power Part 2

Read the graphs on page 263 and answer the questions.

1. What is the difference between the two graphs? _____

2. Do both graphs show the same information? _____

3. What information do the graphs show? _____

4. How many tulips did Madeline plant? _____

5. How many more tulips than sunflowers does Madeline have in her garden?

_____

6. How many flowers did Madeline plant in her garden? _____

7. Explain how Madeline might use the information on the graphs.

_____ _____

Try This!

   A. On the back of this paper, draw a graph of the vegetables you might plant in a garden.

   B. Ask your classmates about their favorite flowers. On another sheet of paper, draw a graph to show the information.

Name: _____

Funny Faces

Read each graph to draw the funny faces.

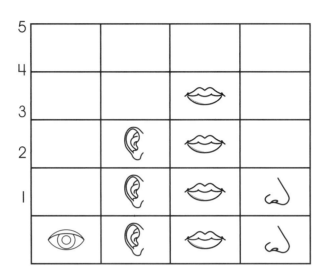

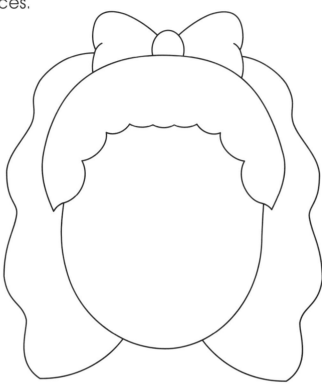

	eye	ear	mouth	nose
5				
4				ca
3				ca
2	eye	ear		ca
1	eye	ear	mouth	ca

eye ear mouth nose

A. On the back of this paper, draw a silly face. Then, draw a grid like the one above and make a line graph of your drawing.

B. On another sheet of paper, write a descriptive paragraph about one of the funny faces created on this page.

265

Name: _____

Candle Sale Part 1

Lincoln Elementary School is selling candles as a fund-raiser. Complete the bar graph to show the number of candles sold at each grade level. Then, answer the questions on page 267.

Candle Sale Totals

Grade	Number Sold	Grade	Number Sold
K	47	3	68
I	79	4	55
2	32	5	82

Candle Sale Totals

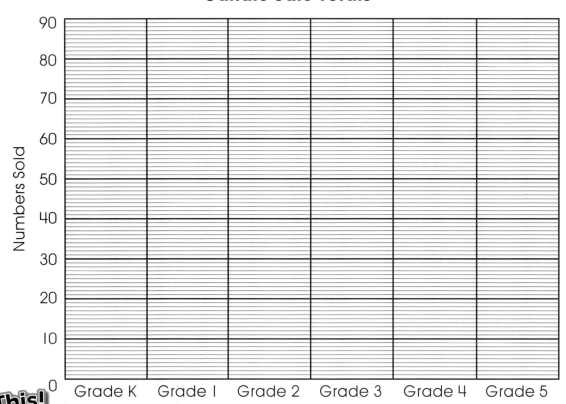

Try This!

A. On the back of this paper, write how you decided where to put the number 47 on the graph.

B. Choose five friends or family members. Then, graph their ages on a graph like the one above.

Candle Sale Part 2

Read the graph on page 266 and answer the questions.

1. What does the graph show? _____

2. Which grade sold the most candles? _____

3. Which grade sold the least number of candles? _____

4. Did the primary grades (K, 1, and 2) sell more or fewer than the upper grades

   (3, 4, and 5)? _____ By how much? _____

5. How many candles did the students at Lincoln Elementary sell in all? _____

6. What information does the graph *not* show? _____

A. On the back of this paper, draw a picture graph of the same information from page 267.

B. Imagine that your class sold the most candles and won a party as a reward. On another sheet of paper, write a story about winning the contest and the party afterward.

Hot Lunch Favorites

Banks asked 32 of his friends to name their favorite school lunches. He showed the information in a circle graph. Read the circle graph. Then, answer the questions.

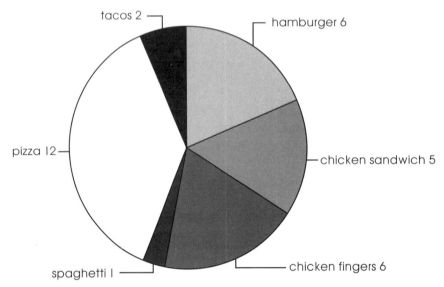

1. Which food is the favorite? _____

2. Which two foods are the least favorite? _____

3. Which three foods were close in number of votes? _____

_____

_____

4. How many students did Banks survey? _____

5. What recommendations would you make to the cafeteria staff after reading the

   information on the graph? _____

6. What information is *not* provided on this graph? _____

A. Survey your classmates about their favorite school lunches. On the back of this paper, create a circle graph of the information.

B. Write a letter to the cafeteria staff at Banks' school to tell them about the information Banks learned by taking the survey and creating a graph.

What a Pair!

Write the ordered pair for each letter. The first one has been done for you.

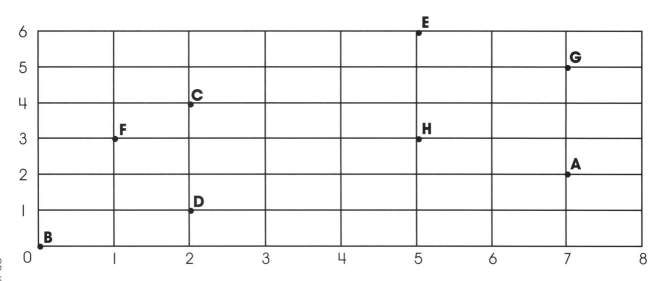

A ____(7,2)____   E _____

B _____   F _____

C _____   G _____

D _____   H _____

A. On the back of this paper, write step-by-step directions for writing an ordered pair.

B. On a sheet of grid paper, make a grid and place eight dots. Then, write an ordered pair to describe each dot.

Interesting Plot

Plot each ordered pair on the grid. Then, connect the dots, in order, to reveal a picture. The first one has been done for you.

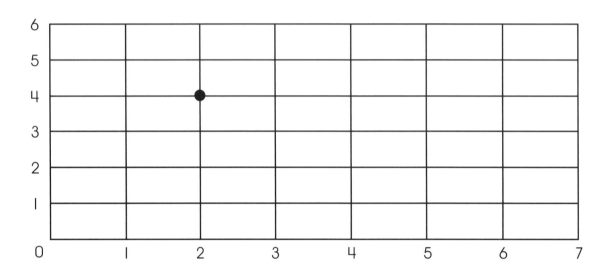

A. (2,4)	H. (7,3)	O. (2,2)
B. (3,4)	I. (6,2)	P. (1,2)
C. (4,4)	J. (5,1)	Q. (0,2)
D. (4,5)	K. (4,0)	R. (0,3)
E. (4,6)	L. (4,1)	S. (0,4)
F. (5,5)	M. (4,2)	T. (1,4)
G. (6,4)	N. (3,2)	U. (2,4)

Try This!

A. On another sheet of paper, make a poster that explains the steps of plotting ordered pairs on a grid.

B. Draw a picture on a sheet of grid paper. Then, label the points as ordered pairs.

Name: _____

Delivery Time!

Write the letter of each ordered pair on the delivery map.

A. (3,0)   B. (4,3)   C. (7,3)   D. (6,6)   E. (9,8)   F. (12,9)

Try This!

A. Use a red crayon to map out a different delivery route on the map above. Mark each stop with an ordered pair.

B. On the back of this paper, explain how it is helpful to know ordered pairs to read a map.

271

What Would You Like?

A restaurant is offering a sandwich, a drink, and a dessert for one low price. Look at the choices on the menu. Then, list at least 12 combinations you could order.

Menu		
Sandwiches	Drinks	Desserts
turkey	milk	oatmeal cookie
avocado	lemonade	apple slices
egg salad	apple juice	yogurt
PB&J	bottled water	granola bar

_____

_____

_____

_____

_____

_____

_____

_____

_____

_____

_____

 **Try This!**

A. On another sheet of paper, list two sandwiches, two drinks, and two desserts. Then, list all of the possible combinations.

B. The menu above offers 64 possible combinations. Can you find a pattern for finding the combinations?

Dress a Superhero

Complete the organizer to find all of the possible superhero costumes.

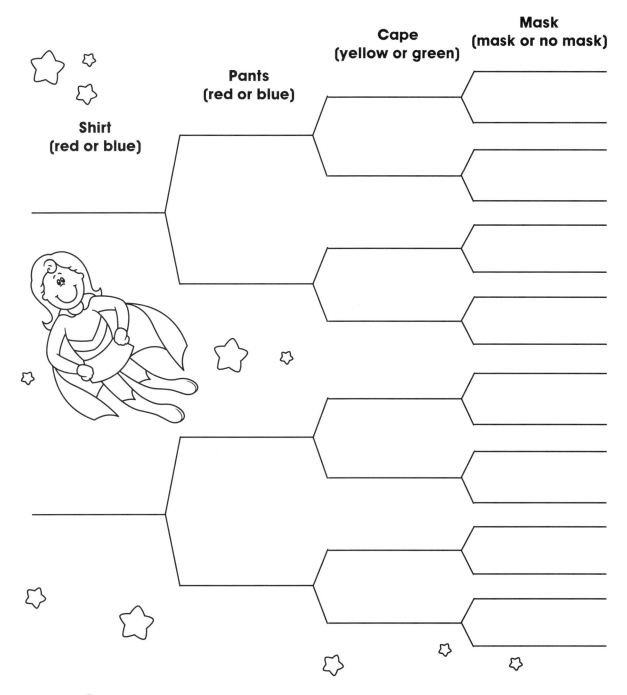

**Shirt
(red or blue)**

**Pants
(red or blue)**

**Cape
(yellow or green)**

**Mask
(mask or no mask)**

Try This!

A. On the back of this paper, draw a picture of the superhero costume you would choose out of the options above.

B. Add boots (yellow or black) to the options for the superhero's costume. On another sheet of paper, draw a new organizer that includes boots. Then, find all of the possible combinations.

The Number Shuffle

Rearrange the numbers 1, 3, and 7 to form all of the possible three-digit numbers. Then, answer the questions.

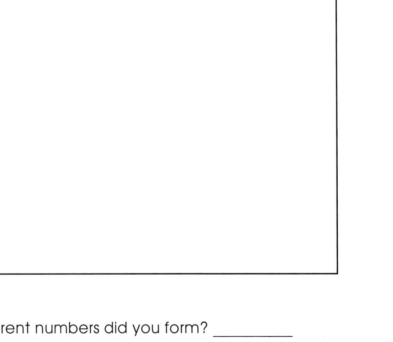

Possible Numbers

1. How many different numbers did you form? _____

2. What was the largest number you formed? _____

3. What was the smallest number you formed? _____

4. What is the difference between the largest and the smallest number? _____

CD-104538 • © Carson-Dellosa

Try This!

A. On the back of this paper, show all of the possible numbers you can form with the digits 4, 7, and 9.

B. On another sheet of paper, show all of the possible numbers you can form with the five digits in your zip code.

What's Your Number?

Rearrange the numbers 4, 6, 8, and 9 to find all of the possible four-digit numbers. Then, find the number that belongs to each student.

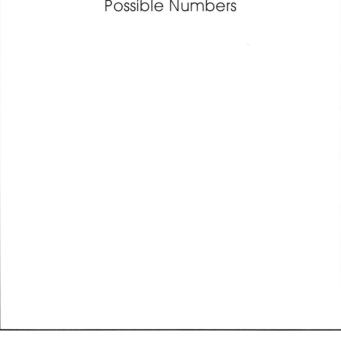

Possible Numbers

1. Lee has the largest number possible. What is Lee's number? _____

2. Shane has the smallest number possible. What is Shane's number? _____

3. Kaylen has the largest number with a 4 in the thousands place.

   What is Kaylen's number? _____

4. Uri has the smallest number possible with the 9 in the tens place.

   What is Uri's number? _____

Try This!

A. Write your phone number on the back of this paper. Arrange the digits to form the largest number possible. Then, arrange the digits to form the smallest number possible.

B. A palindrome is a word or a number that is the same whether it is written backward or forward. For example: mom or 7,227. On another sheet of paper, list as many palindromes as you can think of.

Likely or Unlikely?

Read each sentence. Circle the word that best describes how likely each event is.

1. You will go to school today.   likely   unlikely

2. The sun will rise.   likely   unlikely

3. Your teacher will change into a goose.   likely   unlikely

4. A dinosaur will be at school tomorrow.   likely   unlikely

5. You will complete this page.   likely   unlikely

6. You will walk home from school.   likely   unlikely

7. Your desk will walk away.   likely   unlikely

8. Your friend will eat lunch.   likely   unlikely

A. On another sheet of paper, list five events that are likely and five events that are unlikely.

B. Rewrite each sentence above so that the correct response would be opposite from what it is now.

What's in a Name?

Answer the questions using the tiles shown.

1. What is the probability of choosing an *M*? _____

2. What is the probability of choosing an *L*? _____

3. What is the probability of choosing a vowel? _____

4. What is the probability of choosing a consonant? _____

5. What is the probability of choosing an *A*? _____

6. What is the probability of choosing an *R*? _____

7. What is the probability of choosing a vowel? _____

8. What is the probability of choosing a consonant? _____

A. Write the letters in your name on individual pieces of paper. Place the pieces in a hat and pull them out one at a time. Keep a tally of the letters you draw.

B. Write the days of the week. Then, find the probability of drawing out each day's name.

In the Bag

Look at the prizes in the grab bag. Then, answer the questions.

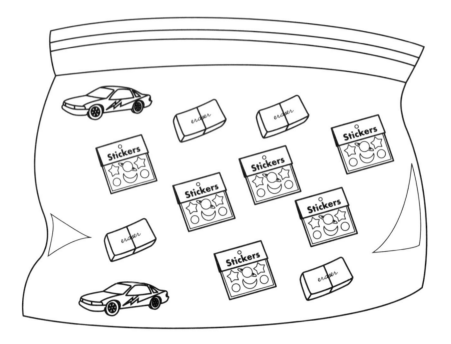

1. What is the probability of pulling out a sticker?

   Write the probability as a fraction. _____

2. What is the probability of pulling out an eraser?

   Write the probability as a fraction. _____

3. What is the probability of pulling out a car?

   Write the probability as a fraction. _____

4. Which prize are you most likely to draw? _____

5. Which prize are you least likely to draw? _____

A. How is the probability of drawing a sticker different from that of the other prizes? Explain on the back of this paper.

B. Rewrite each probability as a ratio on the back of this paper.

Fall in Line

Read each problem. Make a list of all of the possible solutions.

1. Lin, Shelby, and Quan are in line at the water fountain. In what different orders could they be standing?

2. Lin, Shelby, Quan, and Paul are in line. If Paul is always first, and Shelby is always second, how many different ways could the children line up?

3. Lin, Shelby, and Quan are in line in order from shortest to tallest. Shelby is taller than Lin. Quan is shorter than Shelby but taller than Lin. In what order are they standing?

4. Lin, Shelby, Quan, and Paul are in line. How many different ways can they line up if Lin is always first?

A. On another sheet of paper, write your own word problem that requires making a list to solve it.

B. On the back of this paper, make a list of other problems you could solve by making a list.

CD-104538 • © Carson-Dellosa

What to Wear?

Michael cannot decide what to wear to school. Using the items from his closet, make a list of all of the possible outfits he could wear.

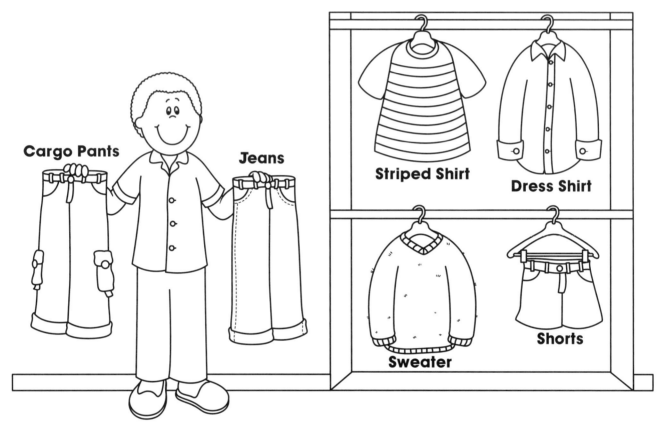

Cargo Pants **Jeans** **Striped Shirt** **Dress Shirt** **Sweater** **Shorts**

CD-104538 • © Carson-Dellosa

_____ _____ _____ _____

_____ _____ _____ _____

_____ _____ _____ _____

_____ _____ _____ _____

_____ _____ _____ _____

Try This!

A. Choose your favorite outfit for Michael. On another sheet of paper, draw a picture of him dressed in that outfit.

B. List some items of clothing from your closet. Then, make a list of possible outfits on another sheet of paper.

Funny Factory

Read each problem. Draw a picture to help you solve it.

1. The Funny Factory puts 5 pieces of trick gum in each pack. How many pieces of gum are in 4 packs?

2. The Funny Factory places 54 hand buzzers evenly into 9 boxes. How many buzzers are in each box?

3. Tyrone ordered 6 boxes of goofy glasses, but he returned 2 boxes. If 2 goofy glasses are in each box, how many goofy glasses did he keep?

4. Ansley wanted to buy some fake teeth. She had $10.00. Each package of fake teeth cost $0.75. How many packages of fake teeth could she buy?

A. On the back of this paper, write three more word problems about the Funny Factory. Draw a picture to show how to solve each problem.

B. Draw a picture to show how drawing a picture can help solve problems.

Fence It In

Read each problem. Draw a picture to help you solve it.

1. Aaron got a new puppy and needs to build a fence around his backyard. His backyard is rectangular. One side is 25 yards wide, and another side is 40 yards long. How many feet of fencing does he need?

2. Joanna needs to replace one side of her fence. If her backyard is square with a total perimeter of 48 yards, how many feet of fencing does she need to replace just one side?

3. Javier has a fence around his swimming pool in the shape of a pentagon. All sides are the same length. If one side is 7 yards long, how many yards of fencing are around his pool?

4. Vanessa has a fence around her backyard that is 12 feet by 15 feet by 12 feet by 15 feet. Her neighbor has a fenced backyard right next to hers that is 12 feet by 20 feet by 12 feet by 20 feet. What is the perimeter around both backyards?

A. On a sheet of grid paper, draw a picture of your dream backyard. Be sure to include the measurements around it.

B. Why do some people think that drawing a picture makes a math problem easier to solve? Explain on another sheet of paper.

CD-104538 • © Carson-Dellosa

Bake Sale!

Read each problem. Use the table to help you solve it.

1. Kelly sold 10 cookies on Monday, 20 cookies on Tuesday, and 30 cookies on Wednesday. If this pattern continues, how many cookies will Kelly sell on Saturday?

Mon.	Tues.	Wed.	Thurs.	Fri.	Sat.

2. In 3 boxes are 60 cookies. In 4 boxes are 80 cookies. How many cookies are in 6 boxes?

3	4	5	6

3. One case has 8 boxes of cookies in it. How many boxes of cookies are in 5 cases?

1	2	3	4	5

4. Laura works at the bake sale for three days and then takes one day off. If she works on the 1st, 2nd, and 3rd, is she going to work on the 14th?

1st	2nd	3rd	4th	5th	6th	7th
8th	9th	10th	11th	12th	13th	14th

A. On another sheet of paper, write three new problems. Use a table to help you solve the problems.

B. Imagine that your school is having a bake sale. What kind of math will you use during the bake sale? Make a list on the back of this paper.

Going on a Picnic

Use the tables to help you solve the problems.

1. Four ants—Anton, Greg, Fiona, and Brady—were carrying food back to the colony. They had an apple, a grape, a banana, and an orange. Anton did not carry anything round. Greg only likes red items. Brady does not like orange juice. What item did Anton, Greg, Fiona, and Brady each carry?

	apple	grape	banana	orange
Anton				
Greg				
Fiona				
Brady				

2. Kit, Liza, Luke, and Jimmy went on a picnic. They each brought a dish to share. Kit did not bring chicken or pizza. Jimmy loves pizza, but Luke does not like salad. Liza brought tamales. What dish did each person bring?

	salad	pizza	chicken	tamales
Kit				
Liza				
Luke				
Jimmy				

A. On another sheet of paper, draw a picture of each person and ant at the picnic with his or her food.

B. On another sheet of paper, write about how a table can help you solve some problems like the ones above.

CD-104538 • © Carson-Dellosa

Library Lessons

Read each problem. Use guess and check to help you solve it.

1. Jill opened a book. The pages she opened to were between 50 and 60. The sum of the two page numbers was 109. What pages did she open to?

2. Molly dropped a book on the floor. It opened to pages that were between 800 and 900. The sum of the two consecutive pages was 1,611. What pages did the book open to?

3. Taylor left his bookmark in his book. He left it somewhere between pages 200 and 300. The sum of the two page numbers is 597. Between which two pages is his bookmark?

4. Sam hid a dollar between two pages of his book. The two pages are between 900 and 1,000. The sum of the two page numbers is 1,829. Between which two pages did he hide the dollar?

A. Open a book to any two pages. On the back of this paper, write a problem about the two page numbers. Challenge a friend to solve your problem.

B. On another sheet of paper, design a bookmark that shows some problem-solving strategies.

Brown-Bag Special

Read each problem. Use guess and check to help you solve it.

1. Nina put the numbers 291, 333, 453, and 563 into a bag. She pulled two numbers out of the bag. The sum of the two numbers is 744, and the difference is 162. What are the two numbers?

2. Paul put the numbers 1,210; 1,009; and 1,154 in a bag. He pulled two numbers out of the bag. The sum of the two numbers is 2,364, and the difference is 56. What are the two numbers?

3. James put the numbers 10, 12, 21, 17, and 11 in a bag. He pulled three numbers out of the bag. The sum of the three numbers is 42. Two of the numbers are odd, and one is even. What are the three numbers?

4. Grace pulled two numbers out of a bag. The sum of the two numbers is 1,419, and the difference is 1. What are the two numbers?

A. On another sheet of paper, write a paragraph that explains how to use guess and check to solve word problems.

B. Make a poster that encourages students to use the guess-and-check strategy.

CD-104538 • © Carson-Dellosa

Skateboard Solutions

Read each problem. Look for a pattern to help you solve it.

1. Reese did 5 cool tricks on Monday, 7 cool tricks on Tuesday, and 9 cool tricks on Wednesday. How many tricks will he do on Saturday if this pattern continues?

Mon.	Tues.	Wed.	Thurs.	Fri.	Sat.
5	7	9			

What's the pattern? _____

2. Leigh designed a pattern for the top of her skateboard. She drew a triangle, a square, a triangle, and a square.

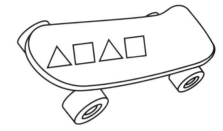

If this pattern continues, what will be the sixth shape she draws?

_____

3. At the skateboard tournament, the scores formed a pattern: 99, 90, 95, 86, and 91. If the pattern continues, what will be the eighth score?

1st	2nd	3rd	4th	5th	6th	7th	8th
99	90	95	86	91			

What is the pattern? _____

4. Brad fell off his skateboard 45 times the first day, 34 times the second day, and 23 times the third day. If this pattern continues, how many times will he fall on the fourth day?

1st	2nd	3rd	4th
45	34	23	

What is the pattern? _____

A. On the back of this paper, draw your own pattern to put on a skateboard.

B. On another sheet of paper, write a story about your friends and skateboarding. Include one pattern in your story.

To the Rescue!

Read each problem. Look for a pattern to help you solve it.

1. A princess made a rope out of jewels. The order of the jewels was ruby, emerald, emerald, ruby, emerald, emerald. If the pattern continues, what will be the 15th jewel she uses?

2. The princess has many jewels in her collection. She has 2 rubies, 4 emeralds, and 16 diamonds. If the next jewels are pearls and the pattern continues, how many pearls does the princess have?

3. The knight's ladder has 25 steps. Each step has a jewel on it. The first step has a diamond. The second step has a ruby. The third step had a ruby, and the fourth step has a diamond. If this pattern continues, what will be the last jewel on the ladder?

Try This!

A. On the back of this paper, draw a jewel necklace with a pattern.

B. On another sheet of paper, write about how patterns can help solve problems.

Shopping Spree

Read each problem. Then, circle the letter or letters of the best answer.

1. Tyrone got some money for his birthday. He spent $49.00 on a video game. He gave a friend $12.00. He also bought a new toy for $15.00. If he had $24.00 left over, how much did he start with?

2. Khalil walked from one side of the toy store to the other. It took him 5 minutes to walk from the video games to the race cars. Then, it took him 7 minutes to walk from the race cars to the board games. He got to the board games at 4:00 P.M. At what time did he leave the video games?

3. Right now, 20 toys are on the shelf. Five minutes ago, Kelly took 7 toys off of the shelf. Ten minutes ago, Luis took 3 toys off of the shelf. How many toys were on the shelf to begin with?

4. Noah spent $53.00 at the toy store. He bought a football for $10.00 and some trading cards for $20.00. He also bought some interlocking blocks. How much did he spend on the blocks?

CD-104538 • © Carson-Dellosa

 **Try This!**

A. Choose one problem from above. On another sheet of paper, draw a picture to show how you solved the problem.

B. Imagine that you won a $100.00 shopping spree at your favorite store. Make a list on the back of this paper of what you would buy.

A Trip to the Amusement Park

Read each problem. Work backward to help you solve it.

1. The Johnson family went to the amusement park. They drove a total of 42 miles. How many miles was it from their house to the park?

2. The Johnson family includes Mr. and Mrs. Johnson and Jason and Jack. If an adult ticket costs $10.00, and a child ticket costs $7.50, how much did they spend on tickets?

3. The Petrovs went to the amusement park too. They left home at 9:00 A.M. and arrived at the park 20 minutes later. They spent 5 hours at the park and then drove home. What time did they get home?

4. Mr. Petrov bought tickets for himself and his children. He spent a total of $40.00 for the tickets. Adult tickets cost $10.00 each, and child tickets cost $7.50 each. How many children does Mr. Petrov have?

CD-104538 • © Carson-Dellosa

 **Try This!**

A. Write a math problem about an amusement park for a family member to solve.

B. Imagine that you are going on a trip somewhere fun. On another sheet of paper, write a paragraph to describe your trip. Include at least one math problem in your story.

Answer Key

Page 9
1. Baker; 2. Barnaby; 3. Casper; 4. Dylan; 5. Harmon; 6. Jersey; 7. Laramie; 8. Leghorn; 9. Lester; 10. Newton; Try This!: answers will vary.

Page 10
1. deep; 2. diver; 3. fins; 4. fish; 5. helmet; 6. mask; 7. ocean; 8. octopus; 9. oxygen; 10. suit; 11. swim; 12. tank; Try This!: answers will vary.

Page 11
1. Brick Fall; 2. Bubble Blower; 3. Café; 4. Cooking; 5. Pet Palaces; 6. Race Rally; 7. Roly-Poly; 8. Zoink; A Post Office! Try This!: answers will vary.

Page 12
bl words: blink, blow, (blip); *fl* words: fly, flip, (flow); *cl* words: clasp, climb, (clip), (clink); Try This!: answers will vary.

Page 13
1. sw; 2. st; 3. tw; 4. st; 5. sw; 6. tw; Try This!: answers will vary.

Page 14
1. scout; 2. mountain; 3. trout; 4. flower; 5. shout; 6. shower; 7. tower; 8. count; Try This!: answers will vary.

Page 15
prowl, scowl; power, tower; bow, brow; down, town; powder, chowder; Try This!: answers will vary.

Page 16
Row 1: thumb, shirt, cheese; Row 2: shoe, thorn, check; Row 3: chin, shell, thermos; Try This!: answers will vary.

Page 17
1. tent; 2. nest; 3. raft; 4. ant; 5. plant; 6. forest; 7. soft; 8. footprint; Try This!: answers will vary.

Page 18
Row 1: couch, brush, mouth; Row 2: wreath, bath, dish. Row 3: bench, fish, cloth; Try This!: answers will vary.

Page 19
grasshopper; skateboard; grandmother; bookshelf; popcorn; doghouse; Try This!: answers will vary.

Page 20
outdoor, doorknob; teacup, cupcake; bedroom, roommate; lifetime, timeline; sidewalk, walkway; Try This!: answers will vary.

Page 21
Answers will vary. Try This!: answers will vary.

Page 22
blue: sun, Earth, Mars, moon, star; red: planet, orbit, Venus, Saturn, Neptune; green: Mercury, Jupiter, Uranus; yellow: constellation, meteorite, astronomer; Try This!: answers will vary.

Page 23
1. jump/ing, 2; 2. hur/dle, 2; 3. out/side, 2; 4. ex/er/cise, 3; 5. suc/cess, 2; 6. bounce, 1; 7. leap, 1; 8. hel/met, 2; 9. back/yard, 2; 10. hop/ping, 2; answers will vary. Try This!: answers will vary.

Page 24
1. I'm; 2. we're; 3. they've; 4. we'll; 5. she's; 6. don't; 7. isn't; 8. it's; 9. you're; 10. haven't; Try This!: answers will vary.

Page 25
1. are not; 2. she will; 3. you are; 4. he is; 5. you will; 6. we are; 7. they are; 8. I am; 9. cannot; Try This!: answers will vary.

Page 26

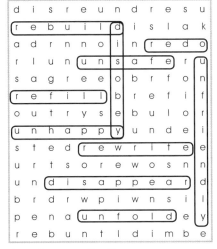

1. unhappy; 2. disobey; 3. unsafe; 4. refill; 5. disappear; 6. rewrite; 7. unfold; 8. redo; 9. unfriendly; 10. rebuild; Try This!: answers will vary.

Page 27
remake; unopened; unknown; unkind; distrust; rewrap; disrespect; Try This!: answers will vary.

Page 28
-er words: teacher, worker, driver; *-ful* words: beautiful, doubtful, thoughtful; *-less* words: colorless, careless, meaningless; Try This!: answers will vary.

Page 29
Across: 1. government; 3. harden; 4. washable; 5. development; 9. shipment; Down: 2. readable; 6. lighten; 7. enjoyable; 8. tighten; Try This!: answers will vary.

Page 30
1. smaller, smallest; 2. stranger, strangest; 3. brighter, brightest; 4. prettier, prettiest; 5. dirtier, dirtiest; 6. biggest; 7. faster; 8. heaviest; 9. coolest; Try This!: answers will vary.

Page 31
1. dis/approve: to not approve of; 2. fool/ish: like a fool; 3. un/sure: not sure; 4. friend/ly: having the quality of a friend;

5. re/pay: to pay back; 6. care/less: without care; 7. hope/ful: with hope; 8. un/wrap: to remove wrapper; Try This!: answers will vary.

Page 32

1. pretty; 2. huge; 3. respect; 4. applaud; 5. get; 6. intelligent; 7. plead; 8. leap; 9. positive; Puzzle answer: YOUR TEETH; Try This!: answers will vary.

Page 33

Try This!: answers will vary.

Page 34

right, wrong; uneven, even; stormy, calm; achieve, fail; approve, dislike; polite, rude; Try This!: answers will vary.

Page 35

unlock and lock; strong and weak; cooked and raw; bad and good; present and absent; sharp and dull; small and big; buy and sell; Try This!: answers will vary.

Page 36

Answers will vary.
Try This!: answers will vary.

Page 37

Synonyms: delicious/tasty; clean/tidy; dirty/filthy; shout/yell; bland/tasteless; large/gigantic; afraid/scared; laugh/giggle; smart/intelligent; thin/slim; Antonyms: front/back; first/last; hot/cold; sloppy/neat; huge/small; hungry/satisfied; Try This!: answers will vary.

Page 38

1. a bare bear; 2. a hoarse horse; 3. a dear deer; 4. a knight night; 5. a weak week; 6. a fair fare; 7. feet feat; 8. aunt ant; Try This!: answers will vary.

Page 39

add, ad; eight, ate; scent, cent; Try This!: answers will vary.

Page 40

1. yes; 2. yes; 3. no; 4. no; 5. yes; 6. no; 7. no; 8. yes; Try This!: answers will vary.

Page 41

1. b. male deer; 2. b. alert or observant; 3. a. beat or pound; 4. a. fight; 5. a. hit; 6. b. look at closely; Try This!: answers will vary.

Page 42

absorption (n); clay (n); compost (n); decompose (v); erosion (n); gravel (n); humidity (n); inorganic (adj); microbe (n); mineral (n); organic (adj); Try This!: answers will vary.

Page 43

1. Look at the guide words. 2. noun, verb, and adjective; 3. two; 4. Answers will vary. 5. compost; 6. science; Answers will vary. 7. Answers will vary. 8. Answers will vary. Try This!: answers will vary.

Page 44

1. lean, leap, leaf; 2. give, glass; 3. ruler, ruin; 4. pyramid, puzzle; 5. act, acronym; 6. silver, similar, simile; Try This!: answers will vary.

Page 45

Have you ever used a compass to find your way? (interrogative) A compass is a magnet that can identify geographic direction. (declarative) It is easy to make your own compass, and it is a lot of fun too! (exclamatory) First, you will need to make a sewing needle magnetic.

(declarative) To do this, pull the needle toward you across a magnet several times. (imperative) Be sure to pull the needle in the same direction each time. (imperative) Once the needle is magnetic, tape it to a small piece of plastic. (imperative) Then, float the needle in a dish of water. (imperative) Wait for your floating needle to stop spinning. (imperative) In what direction is it pointing? (interrogative) What happens to the needle? (interrogative) Try This!: answers will vary.

Page 46

Our class did an experiment with plants. (declarative) Wow, look at those plants grow! (exclamatory) Why isn't the plant growing in the dark? (interrogative) Water the plants every day. (imperative) What would happen if we fed the plants juice? (interrogative) It was so much fun doing a science experiment! (exclamatory) Record all data carefully. (imperative) Next time, we will see how plants grow with music. (declarative) Try This!: answers will vary.

Page 47

1. NASA built a spacecraft called *Apollo 11*, and they launched it on July 16, 1969. 2. Four days later, *Apollo 11* reached the moon, and on July 20, Neil Armstrong and Buzz Aldrin walked on the moon. 3. The astronauts took many pictures of the moon, but they also collected 47 pounds of moon rocks. 4. You can read about their moonwalk online, or you can read about it in history books. Try This!: answers will vary.

Answer Key

Page 48

1. work; 2. solve; 3. lose; 4. loses; 5. writes; 6. use; 7. keep; 8. know; Try This!: answers will vary.

Page 49

Answers will vary. Try This!: answers will vary.

Page 50

present tense: twinkle, shoot, move, rise; past tense: sparkled, gazed, counted, looked; future tense: will shine, will watch, will fade, will name; Try This!: answers will vary.

Page 51

1. became, will become; 2. rode, will ride; 3. came, will come; 4. drew, will draw; 5. gave, will give; 6. drove, will drive; 7. took, will take; 8. won, will win; Try This!: answers will vary.

Page 52

Answers will vary. Try This!: answers will vary.

Page 53

Answers will vary. Try This!: answers will vary.

Page 54

1. he; 2. She; 3. We; 4. They; 5. them; 6. him; 7. It; 8. her; Try This!: answers will vary.

Page 55

Answers will vary. Try This!: answers will vary.

Page 56

Answers will vary. Try This!: answers will vary.

Page 57

children; cities; sheep; knives; rashes; feet; cars; mice; ponies; halves; couches; dresses; Try This!: answers will vary.

Page 58

Answers will vary. Try This!: answers will vary.

Page 59

Answers will vary. Try This!: answers will vary.

Page 60

1. X ; "After lunch," said Reba, "let's go shopping." 2. X; Taron goes to Hudson Elementary School in Forest Park. 3. C; 4. X; We saw the movie "Sub Sandwich Sleuths" yesterday. 5. C; 6. X; The Hansens live in Los Angeles, California. Try This!: answers will vary.

Page 61

Answers will vary. Try This!: answers will vary.

Page 62

1. Young Abraham was a happy, calm, and intelligent child. 2. His parents paid his teacher with firewood, venison, and potatoes. 3. Abe liked to tell jokes, stories, and tall tales. 4. Abe loved to read, write, and talk with people. 5. Abe worked as a storekeeper, a surveyor, a boatman, and a postmaster. 6. He and his wife enjoyed music, dancing, and the theater. 7. Their four sons were named Robert, Edward, Willie, and Tad. 8. President Lincoln helped free the slaves, unite the North and South, and keep the country united. Try This!: answers will vary.

Page 63

Answers will vary. Try This!: answers will vary.

Page 64

1. Pilar created her own country. 2. She created her country on October 29, 2011. 3. What would her country be like? 4. What would be the law of the land? 5. She wanted all citizens to be equal. 6. Men, women, and children would have the same rights. 7. All races, religions, and cultures would be respected. 8. Everyone would live in peace. Try This!: answers will vary.

Page 65

January 20, 2011
Dearest Mother,

I arrived in America safely. It is a very beautiful country with lovely mountains, trees, and blue skies. I even saw a deer in the woods.

Yesterday, I helped Aunt Sarah plant a garden. We planted corn, beans, and carrots. I can't wait to taste the vegetables.

Tell Father, Matthew, and Jonathan that I send my love. I miss you greatly and will write again soon.

Love,
Nellie

Try This!: answers will vary.

Page 66

1. Juicy Frozen Fruit; 2. Sugar-Free Bubble Gum; 3. Instant Oatmeal; 4. Fruit Bar; 5. All-Natural Ice Cream; 6. Granola Bar; Try This!: answers will vary.

Page 67

1. Amber Walsh hated her name. Without even trying, she could think of 20 better names. In fact, when her family moved to Lakeville, she thought about telling everyone that her name was Madison. She decided it was not a good idea. She might not turn around when someone said, "Madison."
2. One day, Amber read about amber in her science book. She learned that amber is a type of fossil made from tree sap. Some trees with layers of sap on their trunks aged and died. When they fell, they were covered with dirt or water. The trees were buried for millions of years.
Try This!: answers will vary.

Page 68

1. Yesterday, my class visited the zoo. We were amazed at all of the animals that

Answer Key

lived there. Animals from all over the world were in their natural habitats. ~~My natural habitat is a house.~~ My favorite animal was the elephant.

2. We played a game called Silent Ball. To play this game, everyone must stand in a circle and be very quiet. A sponge ball is then passed from person to person. The ball may be passed to a person next to you or to a person across the room. ~~Miranda does not like the game, so she chose not to play.~~ If a player misses the ball or makes a sound, he must sit down. The last person standing is the winner.

3. Jose has an unusual pet. It is an iguana named Spike. Spike lives in a glass house made from an old fish aquarium. He eats a special diet of fruit and green plants. Spike has a greenish-gray color and blends into his environment. ~~My friend Mario has an unusual pet too.~~ Jose's unusual pet is fun to observe.
Try This!: answers will vary.

Page 69
Topic sentence: The wind spreads seeds. Detail sentences: Dandelion seeds have parachutes. Maple seeds have wings. The wind picks up some seeds and carries them. Topic sentence: Animals spread seeds. Detail sentences: Some seeds with spikes attach to animals' fur. Some sticky seeds attach to the feet of some animals. Animals eat seeds and move them to other locations through their waste. Try This!: answers will vary.

Page 70
1. Rabbits like to live together in a group. They dig their burrows like underground apartments where they will always have a lot of neighbors. They help each other take care of their young. When the weather turns cold, they snuggle up together to keep each other warm.

2. The mother and father rabbit scratch a hole in the sandy wall of the burrow with their front feet. Then, they use their back feet to push the loose ground back into the tunnel. The mother rabbit smoothes the walls and then pulls out pieces of her fur to line the floor. Both mother and father rabbit work hard to prepare a nursery for the babies who will soon be born.
Try This!: answers will vary.

Page 71
Alexis and Emma's teacher gave them a research project. Alexis and Emma decided to research the history of money. First, they looked online for important information. Then, Alexis and Emma went to the local library. There they checked out a book called *The History of Money*. Alexis read the book and then told Emma all about it. Emma wrote the information in a report. After the report was written, Alexis and Emma made a display. Finally, the girls presented their report to the class. Try This!: answers will vary.

Page 72
6 Cook the pancakes until they are lightly browned on both sides.
2 In a small bowl, mix together melted butter, egg, and milk.
4 Have an adult help you spoon 1/4 cup of the pancake batter on to a heated skillet.
1 In a large bowl, mix together flour, sugar, baking powder, and salt. Set aside.
5 When bubbles start to appear in the pancake, flip it over with a spatula.
7 Serve the pancakes with your favorite pancake topping and enjoy.
3 Add the egg mixture to the flour mixture. Stir until it is well blended.
Try This!: answers will vary.

Page 73
Take out your toothbrush and toothpaste. Wet the toothbrush with water. Squeeze the toothpaste onto your toothbrush. Brush your top and bottom teeth. Brush your tongue. Spit out the toothpaste and rinse your mouth. Rinse off your toothbrush until it is clean. Wipe your mouth. Put away your toothbrush and toothpaste. Try This!: answers will vary.

Page 74
Answers will vary. Try This!: answers will vary.

Page 75
Answers will vary. Try This!: answers will vary.

Page 76
Traveling in a space shuttle is fun. The astronauts can see Earth from a distance of 160 miles. Because the space shuttle orbits Earth so quickly, they also see several sunrises and sunsets in one day.

They pass over continents and oceans. It is very easy to see the United States and the Pacific Ocean from that distance.

The space shuttle travels around the whole world. It takes pictures and records data to bring back to NASA. The journey is incredible.
Try This!: answers will vary.

Pages 77
Answers will vary. Try This!: answers will vary.

Answer Key

Page 78
Answers will vary. Try This!: answers will vary.

Page 79
Answers will vary, but may include: 1. getting his picture taken; 2. unhappy; 3. photographer; 4. It was tight and uncomfortable. Try This!: answers will vary.

Page 80
1. pajamas; 2. feathers; 3. a match; 4. snowflake; 5. rainbow; Try This!: answers will vary.

Page 81
Setting: Los Angeles, CA, early morning, bedroom; Characters: Jeremy, Jeremy's mom; Theme: Jeremy has never been to the beach. Try This!: answers will vary.

Page 82
Answers will vary. Try This!: answers will vary.

Page 83
Answers will vary. Try This!: answers will vary.

Page 84
_5_ The alum and dirt sink to the bottom of the settling basin.
_3_ From the reservoir, water goes into a mixing basin.
_7_ The clean water is stored in a large storage tank.
_1_ First, raindrops fall into streams, lakes, and rivers.
_8_ Water leaves the storage tank through water mains and reaches your home through your faucets.
_4_ Alum is added to take the dirt out of the water.
_6_ Fluoride and chlorine are added to the water.
_2_ Then, the streams and rivers flow into a reservoir.
Try This!: answers will vary.

Page 85
1. Daisy Lane, Tulip Avenue, Zinnia Road; 2. Zinnia Road and Sunflower Drive; 3. Tulip Avenue or Sunflower Drive; 4. Answers will vary but may include left on Daisy Lane, left on Daffodil Road, right on Zinnia Road, left on Violet Road, house is on left. Try This!: answers will vary.

Page 86
Learn to Draw!: inform; M. C. Escher: inform; Try This!: answers will vary.

Page 87
Dog Tails: entertain; The Daily News: inform; Try This!: answers will vary.

Page 88
Answers will vary but may include: Who? Orville and Wilber Wright; What? invented the airplane; When? 1896–1903 Where? Kitty Hawk, North Carolina; Why? They loved the idea of flying. Try This!: answers will vary.

Page 89
Answers will vary but may include: 1. The baby birds, which were hungry and growing, were cared for by their mother. 2. Chirpy liked to jump near the edge of the nest. 3 Chirpy got too close to the edge one day and slipped, but his mother saved him. Try This!: answers will vary.

Page 90
Answers will vary. Try This!: answers will vary.

Page 91
1. F; 2. O; 3. F; 4. F; 5. O; 6. F; 7. O; 8. F; 9. O; 10. O; Try This!: answers will vary.

Page 92
1. Olivia; 2. Felipe; 3. Felipe; 4. Olivia; 5. Olivia; 6. Felipe; 7. Olivia; 8. Felipe; Try This!: answers will vary.

Page 93
1. When the rain started, the boys ran for shelter.
2. Mother served cake after dinner because it was Malia's birthday.
3. Because I cannot swim, my dad will not let me go to the lake by myself.
4. Kevin cannot go to school because he is sick.
5. Nicole went to the movies this afternoon because she was bored.
6. I was so tired that I went to bed early last night.
7. I earned an A on my test because I studied.
8. I skinned my knee when I fell off my bike.
Try This!: answers will vary.

Page 94
1. D; 2. A; 3. F; 4. E; 5. B; 6. G; 7. C; 8. H; Try This!: answers will vary.

Page 95
1. cause; 2. effect; 3. effect; 4. cause; 5. effect; 6. cause; 7. cause; 8. effect; 9. effect; 10. cause; Try This!: answers will vary.

Page 96
Millennium: green; Corkscrew: blue, yellow box, circled; Lightning: blue; Thunderbolt: red, circled; Anaconda: green, purple line; Copperhead: red, yellow box, circled; Avalanche: red, purple line, X; Mountain: blue; Thrill: nothing; Flashback: blue, purple line, circled; Speedy: blue; Hair-Raiser: red, purple line, circled; Splash: nothing; Twisted: blue; Backlash: blue, purple line, circled; Try This!: answers will vary.

Page 97
1. eyes on the dragonfly; 2. six spots on the ladybug; 3. design on the butterfly's wings; 4. five yellow-and-black bees added; 5. two legs added to the spider; 6. grasshopper colored green; 7. picture colored; Try This!: answers will vary.

Answer Key

Page 98

Answers will vary. Try This!: answers will vary.

Page 99

1. nonfiction; 2. to inform; Try This!: answers will vary.

Page 100

1. fiction; 2. to entertain; 3. Frogs and Toads; Try This!: answers will vary.

Page 101

Answers will vary but may include: 1. planet nearest the sun; 2. No. It is too hot on one side and cold on the other. 3. It was named after the Roman messenger for the gods because it moves quickly around the sun. Try This!: answers will vary.

Page 102

Answers will vary but may include: 1. Second from the sun; 2. No, it is too hot. 3. It was named after the Roman goddess of love and beauty. 4. Venus is only hot. Mercury is hot and cold. Venus has thick clouds. Try This!: answers will vary.

Page 103

1. Yellow: They are some of the best insect hunters. Bats help flowers and spread seeds. 2. Blue: More than 900 different kinds of bats; 3. Red: Although most bats eat only insects, some eat fruit and the nectar of flowers. 4. They can measure more than 16 inches (40.6 cm) long. Try This!: answers will vary.

Page 104

1. Hibernation is a long sleep that some animals go into for the winter. 2. Animals get energy from food. 3. They store the food as fat for winter when they hibernate. 4. Their bodies live on the stored fat. Try This!: answers will vary.

Page 105

1. Because the Earth is tilted, 2, 3; 2. warmer and longer, 5, 6; 3. winter, 7, 8, 9; 4. cooler and shorter, 7, 8, 9; Try This!: answers will vary.

Page 106

1. soft inner bark and bushes; 2. around streams; 3. lodge; 4. Answers will vary but may include building dams. Try This!: answers will vary.

Page 107

Check that coloring and circling are correct. 1. Maria and Lucy; 2. the water park; 3. lazy river, wave pool, water slide, ate food; 4. last summer; 5. they won free tickets

Page 108

Answers will vary. Try This!: answers will vary.

Page 109

Answers will vary. Try This!: answers will vary.

Page 110

1. ~~plants~~, cactus, ~~desert plants~~; 2. ~~my life~~, ~~birthdays~~, my best birthday; 3. ~~planets~~, Mars, ~~solar system~~; 4. ~~board games~~, ~~games~~, how to play checkers; 5. ~~school~~, ~~teachers~~, my favorite subject; 6. the best ice cream flavor, ~~desserts~~, ~~sweets~~; Try This!: answers will vary.

Page 111

Answers will vary. Try This!: answers will vary.

Page 112

Answers will vary. ~~Seat belts are important.~~ Try This!: answers will vary.

Page 113

Skateboard for Sale
Black-and-white skateboard with royal blue wheels for sale. Like new. ~~It was my favorite board ever. I need to sell it before I can buy in-line skates.~~ Also comes with cool stickers. Cost is $8.00. Call 555-0123.

~~I am selling my favorite bike. I got it for my sixth birthday.~~ The bike is blue with white stripes. Looks like new. ~~I took really good care of it.~~ Comes with a light and a basket. Cost is $15.00 or best offer. Call 555-0123. Try This!: answers will vary.

Page 114

Answers will vary. Try This!: answers will vary.

Page 115

Answers will vary. Try This!: answers will vary.

Page 116

Answers will vary. Try This!: answers will vary.

Page 117

Answers will vary. Try This!: answers will vary.

Page 118

Blue: the farmer, a little girl; Yellow: worked a long time, opened the lock; Green: in the morning, at night; Red: in the forest, outside; Orange: because it was pretty, to make everyone happy; Try This!: answers will vary.

Page 119

Penguins: Life in Antarctica (nonfiction); *Perry Penguin: Private Investigator* (fiction); *Shake, Rattle, and Roll: Famous Earthquakes* (nonfiction); *Night of the Quakes* (fiction); *Moo! A Cow Joke Book* (fiction); *Moo! The Life of a Cow* (nonfiction); Try This!: answers will vary.

Page 120

1. historical fiction; 2. realistic fiction; 3. historical fiction; 4. realistic fiction; Try This!: answers will vary.

Page 121

1. fairy tale; 2. folktale; 3. not a tale; 4. fairy tale; 5. tall tale; Try This!: answers will vary.

Page 122

1. angry; It's so unfair! Nobody asked me if I wanted to move. 2. She feels better; Well, my

Answer Key

new school is not so bad. 3. friendly; answers will vary. Try This!: answers will vary.

Page 123
Answers will vary. Try This!: answers will vary.

Page 124
Answers will vary. Try This!: answers will vary.

Page 125
Answers will vary. Try This!: answers will vary.

Page 126
Answers will vary. Try This!: answers will vary.

Page 127
Answers will vary. Try This!: answers will vary.

Page 128
Answers will vary. Try This!: answers will vary.

Page 129
Camping can be so much fun. **Last** weekend ~~me and~~ my family **and I** went camping in a park near the **mountains**. We took a lot of stuff because we weren't sure what we would need. Dad and I set up the tents, while Mom and my brother built a campfire and **made** lunch. After lunch, we went swimming in the lake. Later, we went fishing. **My** dad **caught** five fish! He cleaned **them** and cooked them over the campfire for **dinner**. They tasted **great**! After dinner, we **toasted** marshmallows and **told** scary **stories**. I wasn't really afraid. Finally, we crawled inside our tents to go to sleep. It was **quiet** except for the crickets. The next morning, we got up and **started** another day of fun. I love camping**!** Try This!: answers will vary.

Page 130
Last year was **a lot** of fun. In **January**, we went skiing in **Denver,** Colorado. In **February**, my class performed a play about the life of **Martin** Luther **King, Jr**. I got to play the part of **Dr. King**. In the spring, my family spent a **week** at the **beach**. We **saw** two baby sharks **swimming** around the fishing pier! During the summer, I visited my **grandparents** in Texas. I visited the **Space Center** in **Houston**. Finally, in **December**, I had the best birthday ever! I got a puppy. I named him **Wolf** because he looks like a baby wolf. Last year was **really** a lot of fun. I hope next year will be even better! Try This!: answers will vary.

Page 131
Autumn is my favorite time of year. **In September**, the leaves begin to change colors**,** and it starts to get chilly at night. **My** dog, **Ranger**, likes to jump in the piles of **leaves**. **Mom** makes hot chocolate to take to the football game. **We** like to watch the team from **Central High School. They** are the **Red Raiders**. **Go Red Raiders! It** is time for the pumpkin harvest in **October.** Do you like pumpkins**? My** little sister thinks they are funny looking. In **November**, we drive into the town of Evansville **because** they have a big parade. **My Uncle Bob** lets my sister sit on his shoulders so that she can see everything. She is so lucky**! That's** OK **because** I always get to have the first piece of pie at **dinner**. **I** hope you can see why I like autumn. **What** is your **favorite** season**?**

Page 132
My little brother makes me crazy! **Why** did I even have to have a brother**?** He only causes **trouble. He** cries**,** breaks things**,** and runs after the dog. Our house was quiet when he **wasn't** around. But, he does **make** me laugh. Like the time he was **chasing** the dog, and the dog **stopped** and started to chase him. He laughed and laughed. That kid has a **great** laugh. **Our whole** family was laughing. I **guess** he is fun sometimes**.** I also like to read **stories** to him. He thinks I'm really smart**.** I guess that kid isn't so bad. I just wish he **wasn't** so loud when I'm trying to **write** a **paper**. Try This!: answers will vary.

Page 133
Answers will vary. Try This!: answers will vary.

Page 134
Answers will vary. Try This!: answers will vary.

Page 135
Answers will vary. Try This!: answers will vary.

Page 136
Answers will vary. Try This!: answers will vary.

Page 137
Answers will vary. Try This!: answers will vary.

Page 138
Answers will vary. Try This!: answers will vary.

Page 139
Answers will vary. Try This!: answers will vary.

Page 140
Answers will vary. Try This!: answers will vary.

Page 141
Answers will vary. Try This!: answers will vary.

Page 142
Answers will vary. Try This!: answers will vary.

Page 143
Answers will vary. Try This!: answers will vary.

Page 144
Answers will vary. Try This!: answers will vary.

Answer Key

Page 145
Answers will vary. Try This!: answers will vary.

Page 146
Answers will vary. Try This!: answers will vary.

Page 147
Answers will vary. Try This!: answers will vary.

Page 148
Answers will vary. Try This!: answers will vary.

Page 149
Answers will vary. Try This!: answers will vary.

Page 150
1. 29; 2. 135; 3. 70; 4. 864 ; 5. 975; 6. 324; 7. 60; 8. 18; Try This!: answers will vary.

Page 151
1. E; 2. G; 3. A. 4. B; 5. I; 6. C; 7. H; 8. D; 9. F; 10. J; Try This!: answers will vary.

Page 152
1. 9 tens, 1 ones; 2. 1 thousands, 9 hundreds, 8 tens, 9 ones; 3. 3 thousands, 5 hundreds, 1 tens, 4 ones; 4. 4 thousands, 3 hundreds, 2 tens, 1 ones; 5. 3 hundreds, 0 tens, 6 ones; 6. 1 thousands, 0 hundreds, 2 tens, 3 ones; 7. 1 thousands, 0 hundreds, 0 tens, 8 ones; 8. 9 thousands, 1 hundreds, 5 tens, 0 ones; 9. 6 thousands, 1 hundreds, 0 tens, 3 ones; 10. 2 thousands, 0 hundreds, 7 tens, 0 ones; Try This!: answers will vary.

Page 153

1.3	5	0	2.9		3.8	7	4.5	4
7			5.1	6.6	2		8	
7.7	8	8.2		7		9.2	5	0
9		10.5	1	3	11.2	4		
	12.2			13.9	6	0	14.4	
15.7	0	0		16.8		7		0
	0			17.6	6	4	8	0
	1			1				0

Page 154

Place Value Chart

	ten thousands	thousands	hundreds	tens	ones
1. fifty thousand, two hundred twenty-five	5	0	2	2	5
2. ninety-nine thousand, nine hundred ninety-nine	9	9	9	9	9
3. sixty thousand, four hundred thirty-seven	6	0	4	3	7
4. fifty-six thousand, two hundred two	5	6	2	0	2
5. seven thousand, four hundred sixty	0	7	4	6	0
6. nineteen thousand, three	1	9	0	0	3
7. four thousand, three hundred fifty-one	0	4	3	5	1
8. sixty-eight thousand, fifty-seven	6	8	0	5	7

Try This!: answers will vary.

Page 155
1. 936,700; 2. 200; 3. 64, 102; 4. 315,455; 5. 113,313; 6. 9,504; Labels: Zero in the Tens Place, One in the Ten Thousands Place; Try This!: answers will vary.

Page 156
1. 9,851; 2. 4,205; 3. 5,044; 4. 3,170; 5. 2,345; 6. 5,327; 7. 4,367; 8. 36,743; 9. 10,067; 10. 5,809; Try This!: answers will vary.

Page 157

Try This!: answers will vary.

Page 158
1. seven hundred sixty-three; 2. one thousand nineteen; 3. seven thousand five hundred seventeen; 4. four thousand one hundred two; 5. four hundred sixty-seven; 6. fifty-four thousand three hundred ninety-nine; 7. eleven thousand one hundred eleven; 8. twenty-three thousand fifty-seven; Try This!: answers will vary.

Page 159
1. >; 2. =; 3. <; 4. <; 5. >; 6. =; 7. >; 8. >; 9. <; 10. <; 11. >; 12. >; 13. <; 14. <; Because they are smart "kids"; Try This!: answers will vary.

Page 160
1. <; 2. >; 3. <; 4. <; 5. =; 6. <; 7. <; 8. =; 9. <; 10. <; Try This!: answers will vary.

Page 161
Answers will vary. Try This!: A. Answers will vary; B. 406; 473; 546; 608; 698; 725; 758; 810; 968; 2,164; 2,362; 2,473; 4,596; 5,678; 6,409; 21,056; 54,374; 57,234; 58,740; 96,589

Page 162
Answers will vary. Try This!: answers will vary.

Page 163
938, 905, 869, 586, 570, 506, 403, 296, 234, 120; Try This!: A. 900 + 30 + 8; 900 + 5; 800 + 60 + 9; 500 + 80 + 6; 500 + 70; 500 + 6; 400 + 3; 200 + 90 + 6; 200 + 30 + 4; 100 + 20; B. The 5 in the hundreds place in 14,586 is greater than the 4 in the hundreds place in 14,485.

Page 164

1,383		
2,131	3,085	
4,403	4,374	
4,586	9,487	30,967
59,340	43,405	39,213
65,860	70,958	79,890

Try This!: answers will vary.

Page 165
1. 5,732, 1,240, 932, 921; 2. 9,834, 5,685, 4,723, 960; 3. 4,323, 1,423, 1,238, 753; 4. 8,560, 4,086, 3,486, 235; 5. 3,483, 2,463, 301, 235; 6. 4,967, 3,023, 2,139, 587; 7. 4,672, 3,984, 2,164, 932; 8. 3,710, 1,236, 396, 256; 9. 9,325, 6,150, 4,356, 355; 10. 6,346, 2,356, 908, 823; Try This!: answers will vary.

Answer Key

Page 166

Answers will vary but may include: 1. 11,091, 11,132, 11,225; 2. 10,432, 13,011, 14,009; 3. 54,776, 54,786, 54,889; 4. 88,903, 88,913, 88,923; 5. 4,378, 4,460, 4,560; 6. 21,921, 26,001, 26,050; 7. 4,637, 4,725, 4,731; 8. 5,011, 5,111, 5,113; Try This!: answers will vary.

Page 167

1. 590; 2. 460; 3. 1,720; 4. 2,790; 5. 7,870; 6. 880; 7. 340; 8. 3,950; 9. 1,700; 10. 780; A "sham-poodle"; 11. 900; 12. 800; 13. 700; 14. 3,200; 15. 1,900; 16. 6,100; 17. 4,800; A "bull-dog"; Try This!: answers will vary.

Page 168

1. 82 orange; 2. 77 blue; 3. 51 yellow; 4. 35 red; 5. 96 green; 6. 52 red; 7. 73 orange; 8. 92 yellow; 9. 35 red; 10. 74 green; Try This!: answers will vary.

Page 169

1. 795; 2. 771; 3. 991; 4. 886; 5. 992; 6. 990; 7. 890; 8. 781; 9. 877; 10. 883; 11. 871; 12. 772; Try This!: answers will vary.

Page 170

1. T: 810; 2. O: 813; 3. R: 733; 4. I: 747; 5. H: 675; 6. S: 631; 7. E: 976; 8. N: 919; 9. C: 802; 10. L: 815 Answer to riddle: THIRTEEN COLONIES; Try This!: answers will vary.

Page 171

1. 777; 2. 1,145; 3. 1,008; 4. 1,176; 5. 1,421; 6. 738; 7. 1,202; 8. 1,120; 9. 1,110; 10. 921; Try This!: A. 738; 777; 921; 1,008; 1,110; 1,120; 1,145; 1,176; 1,202; 1,421; B. Answers will vary.

Page 172

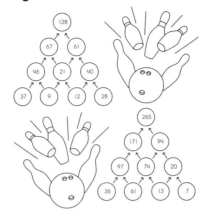

Try This!: A. 37 + 9 = 46; 9 + 12 = 21; 12 + 28 = 40; 46 + 21 = 67; 21 + 40 = 61; 67 + 61 = 128; 36 + 61 = 97; 61 + 13 = 74; 13 + 7 = 20; 97 + 74 = 171; 74 + 20 = 94; 171 + 94 = 265; B. Answers will vary.

Page 173

Estimates will vary. 1. 8,900; 2. 9,851; 3. 9,234; 4. 8,604; 5. 7,771; 6. 8,561; 7. 4,571; 8. 6,924; 9. 5,961. Try This!: answers will vary.

Page 174

1. 12; 2. 22; **3. 12**; 4. 32; **5. 12**; 6. 14; **7. 12**; **8. 12**; Try This!: answers will vary.

Page 175

1. 112; 2. 110; 3. 100; 4. 102; 5. 119; 6. 114; 7. 116; 8. 105; 9. 101; 10. 104; 11. 107; 12. 113; 13. 120; 14. 103; 15. 109; 16. 238; Try This!: answers will vary.

Page 176

1. 195; 2. 92; 3. 45; 4. 93; 5. 191; 6. 181; 7. 185; 8. 265; 9. 171; 10. 183; 11. 74; 12. 161; 13. 120; 14. 761; 15. 180; 16. 156; Try This!: answers will vary.

Page 177

1. 159; 2. 185; 3. 142; 4. 289; **5. 159**; 6. 183; 7. 341; 8. 69; **9. 159**; Try This!: answers will vary.

Page 178

1. 163; 2. 324; 3. 464; 4. 412; 5. 226; 6. 623; 7. 354; 8. 492; 9. 271; Try This!: answers will vary.

Page 179

Across: 1. 725; 3. 517; 4. 326; 6. 384; 8. 645; 10. 429; 12. 319; 14. 715; 16. 624; Down: 1. 747; 2. 583; 3. 543; 5. 206; 7. 459; 9. 489; 11. 255; 13. 176; 15. 108; Try This!: answers will vary.

Page 180

1. B; 2. A; 3. B; 4. C; 5. D; 6. A. 7. B; 8. C; Try This!: A. 41, 6, 73, 36, 140, 14, 250, 108; B. Answers will vary.

Page 181

1. 9; 2. 7; 3. 5; 4. 9, 9; 5. 3; 6. 9; 7. 7, 7; 8. 3, 3; 9. 3, 5; Try This!: answers will vary.

Page 182

1. 2,425; 2. 2,148; 3. 5,246; 4. 3,289; 5. 5,408; 6. 8,209; 7. 2,182; 8. 6,249; 9. 6,428

*	▲	#	◆	•	☺	□	▼	○
2	8	4	0	5	1	6	9	3

Try This!: answers will vary.

Page 183

1. $a=5$; 2. $x=5$; 3. $s=18$; 4. $k=10$; 5. $n=8$; 6. $t=25$; 7. $a=39$; 8. $y=12$; 9. $x=425$; 10. $b=706$; Try This!: answers will vary.

Page 184

1. 36; 2. 5; 3. 40; 4. 4; 5. 63; 6. 3; 7. 52; 8. 6; 9. 297; 10. 27; 11. 117; 12. 224; Try This!: answers will vary.

Page 185

1. 76; 2. 9; 3. 104; 4. 24; Try This!: answers will vary.

Page 186

1. D; 2. H; 3. B; 4. C; 5. F; 6. A. 7. E; 8. G; Try This!: answers will vary.

Page 187

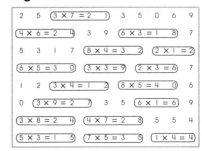

Try This!: answers will vary.

Answer Key

Page 188

36	32	56		63	49		49	63	48	48	63	42	35		42	40	54	48
W	H	O		I	S		S	I	T	T	I	N	G		N	E	X	T

48	56		72	56	81
T	O		Y	O	U	?

Try This!: answers will vary.

Page 189

1. 1, 2, 3, 4, 5, 6, 7, 8, 9, 10, 11, 12;
2. 2, 4, 6, 8, 10, 12, 14, 16, 18, 20, 22, 24; 3. 3, 6, 9, 12, 15, 18, 21, 24, 27, 30, 33, 36; 4. 4, 8, 12, 16, 20, 24, 28, 32, 36, 40, 44, 48; 5. 5, 10, 15, 20, 25, 30, 35, 40, 45, 50, 55, 60; 6. 6, 12, 18, 24, 30, 36, 42, 48, 54, 60, 66, 72; Try This!: answers will vary.

Page 190

7. 7, 14, 21, 28, 35, 42, 49, 56, 63, 70, 77, 84; 8. 8, 16, 24, 32, 40, 48, 56, 64, 72, 80, 88, 96; 9. 9, 18, 27, 36, 45, 54, 63, 72, 81, 90, 99, 108; 10. 10, 20, 30, 40, 50, 60, 70, 80, 90, 100, 110, 120; 11. 11, 22, 33, 44, 55, 66, 77, 88, 99, 110, 121, 132; 12. 12, 24, 36, 48, 60, 72, 84, 96, 108, 120, 132, 144; Try This!: answers will vary.

Page 191

1. 3 horses with 4 legs each = 12 legs in all; 2. 5 spiders with 8 legs each = 40 legs in all; 3. 2 grasshoppers with 6 legs each = 12 legs in all; 4. 4 stools with 3 legs each = 12 legs in all; 5. 6 cows with 4 legs each = 24 legs in all; 6. 7 hens x 2 legs each = 14 in all; Try This!: A. 3 x 4 = 12; 5 x 8 = 40; 2 x 6 = 12; 4 x 3 = 12; 6 x 4 = 24; 7 x 2 = 14; B. Answers will vary.

Page 192

1. 184; 2. 86; 3. 69; 4. 80; 5. 99; 6. 124; 7. 84; 8. 147; 9. 99; 10. 48; 11. 155; 12. 186; Try This!: answers will vary.

Page 193

1. 84; 2. 99; 3. 46; 4. 126; Try This!: answers will vary.

Page 194

1. 2; 2. 1; 3. 8; 4. 3; 5. 4; 6. 0; 7. 6; 8. 5; 9. 9; 10. 7; Try This!: answers will vary.

Page 195

1. 312; 2. 224; 3. 38; 4. 132; 5. 135; 6. 34; 7. 275; 8. 152; 9. 58; 10. 657; 11. 161; 12. 192; 13. 372; 14. 656; Try This!: answers will vary.

Page 196

1. 686; 2. 444; 3. 118; 4. 132; Try This!: answers will vary.

Page 197

1. F; 2. C; 3. G; 4. B; 5. E; 6. H; 7. A. 8. D; Try This!: answers will vary.

Page 198

column 1: 1. 3; 2. 4; 3. 7; 4. 2; 5. 10; 6. 7; 7. 3; 8. 9; 9. 11; 10. 3; 11. 3; 12. 12; 13. 7; 14. 8; column 2: 1. 7; 2. 9; 3. 6; 4. 7; 5. 8; 6. 3; 7. 6; 8. 5; 9. 3; 10. 5; 11. 7; 12. 8; 13. 9; 14. 5; Try This!: answers will vary.

Page 199

12 ÷ 3 = 4, 12 ÷ 4 = 3, 3 x 4 = 12, 4 x 3 = 12; 24 ÷ 6 = 4, 24 ÷ 4 = 6, 6 x 4 = 24, 4 x 6 = 24; 28 ÷ 7= 4, 28 ÷ 4 = 7, 7 x 4 = 28, 4 x 7 = 28; 36 ÷ 9 = 4, 36 ÷ 4 = 9, 9 x 4 = 36, 4 x 9 = 36; 40 ÷ 8 = 5, 40 ÷ 5 = 8, 8 x 5 = 40, 5 x 8 = 40; 63 ÷ 7 = 9, 63 ÷ 9 = 7, 7 x 9 = 63, 9 x 7 = 63; 35 ÷ 7 = 5, 35 ÷ 5 = 7, 7 x 5 = 35, 5 x 7 = 35; 54 ÷ 6 = 9, 54 ÷ 9 =6, 9 x 6 = 54, 6 x 9 = 54; 32 ÷ 8 = 4, 32 ÷ 4 = 8, 8 x 4 = 32, 4 x 8 = 32; Try This!: A. 7 x 6 = 42, 6 x 7 = 42, 42 ÷ 6 = 7, 42 ÷ 7 = 6; B. Answers will vary.

Page 200

1. 6; 2. 6; 3. 7; 4. 5; 5. 8; 6. 4; 7. 9; 8. 7; 9. 9; 10. 6; 11. 7; 12. 7; 13. 5; 14. 3; 15. 8; 16. 5; 17. 6; 18. 7; 19. 9; 20. 5. Try This!: answers will vary.

Page 201

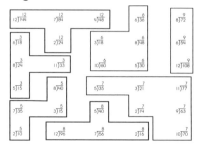

Try This!: answers will vary.

Page 202

1. 2 cookies; 2. 3 dog biscuits; 3. 5 pieces of pepperoni; 4. 6 books. Try This!: answers will vary.

Page 203

1. 13; 2. 11; 3. 12; 4. 13; 5. 18; 6. 33; 7. 13; 8. 10; 9. 15; 10. 16; 11. 19; 12. 31; 13. 42; 14. 22; 15. 14; 16. 17; Try This!: answers will vary.

Page 204

1. 5 r3; 2. 6 r3; 3. 8 r2; 4. 3 r2; 5. 8 r3; 6. 7 r2; 7. 5 r3; 8. 6 r5; 9. 4 r5; Try This!: answers will vary.

Page 205

1. 9 r5; 2. 4 r2; 3. 16 r1; 4. 18 r1; 5. 13 r1; 6. 14 r2; 7. 16 r1; 8. 27 r1; 9. 12 r1; 10. 11 r5; 11. 16 r2; 12. 10 r4; Try This!: answers will vary.

Page 206

E. 7 r2; T. 9 r1; D. 3 r3; S. 7 r4; I. 7 r3; B. 12 r1; U. 5 r3; H. 3 r2; A. 6 r2; N. 6 r1; R. 10 r7; G. 2 r2; Because their students are so bright! Try This!: answers will vary.

Page 207

1. 4 bags; 2. 23 buckets; 3. 44 buckets; 4. 25 cups; 5. Ana; 6. 19 cups. Cody popped fewer than Ana. Try This!: answers will vary.

Page 208

1. x; 2. ÷; 3. −; 4. +; 5. −; 6. +; 7. −; 8. x; 9. − 10. ÷; 11. ÷; 12. x; 13. ÷; 14. −; Try This!: answers will vary.

Page 209

1. B; 2. D; 3. C; 4. C; 5. B; 6. A. Try This!: answers will vary.

Answer Key

Page 210
1. 42¢; 2. 66¢; 3. 97¢; 4. 73¢;
6. 88¢; 6. 80¢; Try This!: answers will vary.

Page 211
1. 1 dollar, 1 dime, 1 nickel, 2 pennies; 2. 2 dollars, 4 pennies; 3. 1 dollar, 3 quarters, 4 pennies; 4. 2 dollars, 1 quarter, 2 dimes, 1 penny or 2 dollars, 4 dimes, 1 nickel, 1 penny; Try This!: answers will vary.

Page 212
1. 1 ten-dollar bill, 1 five-dollar bill, 1 quarter; 2. 1 five-dollar bill, 1 dollar, 1 dime; 3. 1 ten-dollar bill, 1 five-dollar bill, 2 dollars, 1 quarter, 1 dime (or 3 dimes, 1 nickel), 4 pennies; 4. 1 ten-dollar bill, 1 five-dollar bill, 2 dollars, 1 dime, 1 nickel, 1 penny; Try This!: A. $6.10, $15.25, $17.16, $17.39; B. $55.90

Page 213

	Amount	Quarters	Dimes	Nickels	Pennies
1.	$0.76	3	0	0	1
2.	$0.45	1	2	0	0
3.	$0.98	3	2	0	3
4.	$0.40	1	1	1	0
5.	$0.84	3	0	1	4
6.	$0.62	2	1	0	2
7.	$1.42	5	1	1	2
8.	$1.68	6	1	1	3

Page 214
1. $50.42; 2. $43.94; 3. $44.13; 4. $22.79; 5. $51.00; 6. $80.73; 7. $44.45; 8. $65.76; 9. $65.70; Try This!: answers will vary.

Page 215
1. 29.99 + 4.99 = $34.98; 2. 14.50 + 13.00 = $27.50; 3. 15.65 + 4.99 = $20.64; 4. 14.50 + 25.50 = $40.00; 5. 13.00 + 8.99 = $21.99; 6. 29.99 + 15.65 = $45.64; Try This!: answers will vary.

Page 216
1. $19.50; 2. $2.39; 3. $9.16; 4. $12.97; 5. $14.20; 6. $7.49; Try This!: answers will vary.

Page 217
Answers will vary. Try This!: answers will vary.

Page 218
1. $5.45; 2. $5.00; 3. $10.00; 4. $7.75. Try This!: A. $4.55, $5.00, 0, $2.25; B. $10.30, $10.75, $5.75, $8.00

Page 219
puzzle, $2.00; football, $9.00; wind-up car, $20.00; board game, $6.00; baseball, $4.00; blocks, $4.00; video game, $19.00; teddy bear, $17.00; doll, $12.00; Try This!: A. Answers will vary. B. All of the toys would cost $120.00 before the sale and $93.00 during the sale.

Page 220
1. Answers will vary; 2. $7.75; 3. $29.00; 4. $22.79; Try This!: answers will vary.

Page 221

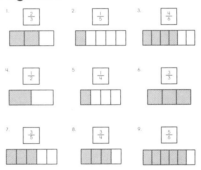

Try This!: A. 1/3, 4/5, 2/6, 1/2, 3/4, 0, 2/5; 1/4; 1/6; B. Answers will vary.

Page 222
1. C; 2. A. 3. D; 4. B; 5. E; Try This!: answers will vary.

Page 223
1/2 = 2/4, 4/8, 3/6; 1/3 = 2/6, 3/9, 4/12; 1/4 = 2/8, 4/16, 3/12; Try This!: answers will vary.

Page 224
1. 2/3 > 1/3; 2. 1/4 = 2/8; 3. 3/8 < 2/3; 4. 3/7 > 3/8; 5. 3/4 < 4/5; 6. 3/6 = 6/12. Try This!: A. Less than 1/2: 1/3, 2/5. More than 1/2: 5/8, 7/9, 6/7, 3/4; Equal 1/2: 3/6, 2/4, 4/8; B. Answers will vary.

Page 225
1. 2/2, 3/3, 4/4, 5/5, 6/6, 8/8; 2. 2/4, 3/6, 4/8; 3. 2/8; Try This!: answers will vary.

Page 226
1. <; 2. <; 3. >; 4. >; 5. >; 6. =; 7. >; 8. >; 9. <; 10. <; Try This!: A. Answers will vary. B. 1/8, 1/6, 1/5, 2/8, 3/10, 1/2, 2/4, 3/6, 4/8, 3/5, 2/3, 7/10, 6/8, 4/5, 10/12, 5/6, 11/12, 2/2, 4/4

Page 227
Answers will vary. Try This!: answers will vary.

Page 228
1. 4 inches; 2. 5 inches; 3. 2 inches; 4. 6 inches; 5. 7 inches; Try This!: A. Answers will vary. B. 1. 10 cm; 2. about 13 cm; 3. 5 cm; 4. 15 cm; 5. about 18 cm

Page 229
1. 3 inches, 8 cm; 2. 3 inches, 7 cm; 3. 4 1/2 inches, 11 cm; 4. 4 inches, 10 cm; 5. 1 inch, 3 cm; 6. 3 1/2 inches, 9 cm; Try This!: answers will vary.

Page 230
1. 36 feet; 2. 60 inches; 3. 2 feet; 4. 72 inches; 5. 216 inches; 6. 4 yards; 7. 48 inches; 8. 63 feet; 9. 3 feet 3 inches; 10. 45 feet or 540 inches; Try This!: answers will vary.

Page 231
1. 4 cups; 2. 8 quarts; 3. 16 cups; 4. 32 pints; 5. 6 cups; 6. 12 cups; 7. 2 gallons; 8. 16 quarts; 9. 2 gallons; 10. 8 pints; Try This!: answers will vary.

Page 232
1. c 2. mL 3. L 4. gal 5. c 6. qt 7.–9. Answers will vary. Try This!: answers will vary.

Page 233
1. ounces; 2. pounds; 3. pounds; 4. tons; 5. pounds; 6. ounces; 7. tons; 8. tons; 9. ounces. Try This!: answers will vary.

Page 234
1. B; 2. H; 3. A. 4. G; 5. C; 6. F; 7. D; 8. E; Try This!: A. 160

Answer Key

ounces; B. Answers will vary.

Page 235
1. 60 inches; 2. 4; 3. 5 ft.; 4. yes; Try This!: answers will vary.

Page 236
1. 212°F, 100°C; 2. 32°F, 0°C; 3. no; 4. yes; 5. yes; 6. ice skate; 7. 78°F; 8. 0°C; Try This!: answers will vary.

Page 237
80°F; 50°C; 30°C; 90°F; Try This!: answers will vary.

Page 238
1. 7:00; 2. 1;30; 3. 2:00; 4. 11:00; 5. 4:30; 6. 12:30; 7. 3:15; 8. 2:45; 9. 9:15; Try This!: answers will vary.

Page 239
Check that times match. Try This!: answers will vary.

Page 240
Check that times match. Try This!: answers will vary.

Page 241

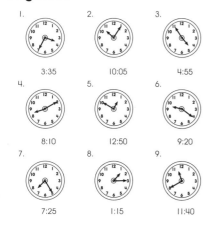

Try This!: A. Answers will vary. B. 86,400 seconds

Page 242
1. 7:00 A.M.; 2. 12:30 P.M.; 3. 2:00 P.M.; 4. 10:20 P.M.; 5. 8:57 P.M.; 6. 8 hours; Try This!: A. twice; B. Answers will vary.

Page 243
1. 6:30, 8:00, 1 hour, 30 minutes; 2. 7:00, 8:45, 1 hour, 45 minutes; 3. 9:10, 5:10, 8 hours; 4. 1:30, 8:15, 6 hours, 45 minutes;

5. 11:00, 3:45, 4 hours, 45 minutes; 6. 2:30, 6:45, 4 hours, 15 minutes; Try This!: answers will vary.

Page 244
1. 9:00 A.M.; 2. 7:25 A.M.; 3. 3:05 P.M.; 4. 3:40 P.M.; 5. 5:00 P.M.; 6. 6:50 P.M.; Try This!: answers will vary.

Page 245
1. 10 square units; 2. 6 square units; 3. 6 square units; 4. 9 square units; 5. 4 square units; 6. 6 square units; Try This!: A. Answers will vary. B. 9

Page 246
Answers will vary. Try This!: answers will vary.

Page 247
1. 24 units; 2. 26 units; 3. 36 units; 4. 28 units; 5. 36 units; Try This!: answers will vary.

Page 248
Answers will vary but should show an understanding of symmetry. Try This!: answers will vary.

Page 249
1. 1; 2. 2; 3. 2; 4. 1; 5. 3; 6. 1; 7. 0; 8. 2; 9. 0; Try This!: answers will vary.

Page 250
1. 3, triangle; 2. 6, hexagon; 3. 4, rectangle; 4. 5, pentagon; 5. 4 square; 6. 0, circle; 7. 4, parallelogram; 8. 8, octagon; 9. 4, rhombus; Try This!: answers will vary.

Page 251
Answers will vary. Try This!: answers will vary.

Page 252
Answers will vary. Try This!: answers will vary.

Page 253
1. right angle; 2. acute angle; 3. obtuse angle; 4. acute angle; 5. obtuse angle; 6. right angle;

7. ; 8. ;

9. ;

Try This!: answers will vary.

Page 254
1. equilateral; 2. isosceles; 3. right; 4. right; 5. equilateral; 6. isosceles; Try This!: answers will vary.

Page 255
1. flip; 2. turn; 3. slide; 4. flip; 5. turn; 6. slide; 7. turn; 8. flip; 9. slide; Try This!: A. Answers will vary. B. flip=reflection, slide=translation, turn=rotation

Page 256
top to bottom: flip; turn; slide; flip; Try This!: answers will vary.

Page 257
1. cube; 2. sphere; 3. cone; 4. square pyramid; 5. rectangular prism; 6. cylinder; Try This!: answers will vary.

Page 258
1. B; 2. D; 3. E; 4. A. 5. C; Try This!: answers will vary.

Page 259
1. cube; 2. rectangular prism; 3. cylinder; 4. square pyramid; Try This!: answers will vary.

Page 260
1. pentagon 2. Answers will vary. 3. cylinder 4. parallel lines; Try This!: answers will vary.

Answer Key

Page 261

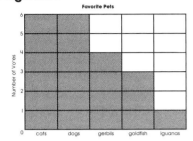

Favorite Pets

Try This!: answers will vary.

Page 262

1. Noah's classmates' favorite pets; 2. 4; 3. iguana; 4. dogs and cats; 5. 7; 6. 3; 7. 20; 8. Answers will vary. Try This!: answers will vary.

Page 263

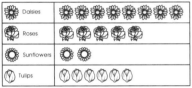

Picture Graph

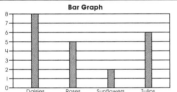

Bar Graph

Try This!: answers will vary.

Page 264

1. One is a picture graph, and one is a bar graph. 2. yes; 3. Flowers Madeline planted in her garden; 4. 6; 5. 4; 6. 21; 7. Answers will vary. Try This!: answers will vary.

Page 265

Answers will vary. Try This!: answers will vary.

Page 266

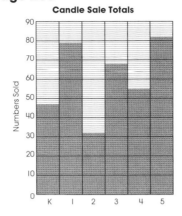

Candle Sale Totals

Try This!: answers will vary.

Page 267

1. The number of candles sold per grade level; 2. fifth grade; 3. second grade; 4. fewer, 47; 5. 363 candles; 6. Answers will vary. Try This!: answers will vary.

Page 268

1. pizza; 2. tacos and spaghetti; 3. hamburgers, chicken sandwich, and chicken fingers; 4. 32; 5. Answers will vary. 6. Answers will vary. Try This!: answers will vary.

Page 269

A. (7,2); B. (0,0); C. (2,4); D. (2,1); E. (5,6); F. (1,3); G. (7,5); H. (5,3); Try This!: answers will vary.

Page 270

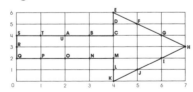

Try This!: answers will vary.

Page 271

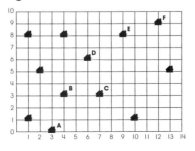

Try This!: answers will vary.

Page 272

Possible combinations: turkey, milk, oatmeal cookie; turkey, lemonade, oatmeal cookie; turkey, apple juice, oatmeal cookie; turkey, water, oatmeal cookie; turkey, milk, apple slices; turkey, lemonade, apple slices; turkey, apple juice, apple slices; turkey, water, yogurt; turkey, milk, yogurt; turkey, lemonade, yogurt; turkey, apple juice, yogurt; turkey, water, yogurt; turkey, milk, granola bar; turkey, lemonade, granola bar; turkey, apple juice, granola bar; turkey, water, granola bar; avocado, milk, oatmeal cookie; avocado, lemonade, oatmeal cookie; avocado, apple juice, oatmeal cookie; avocado, water, oatmeal cookie; avocado, milk, apple slices; avocado, lemonade, apple slices; avocado, apple juice, apple slices; avocado, water, yogurt; avocado, milk, yogurt; avocado, lemonade, yogurt; avocado, apple juice, yogurt; avocado, water, yogurt; avocado, milk, granola bar; avocado, lemonade, granola bar; avocado, apple juice, granola bar; avocado, water, granola bar; egg salad, milk, oatmeal cookie; egg salad, lemonade, oatmeal cookie; egg salad, apple juice, oatmeal cookie; egg salad, water, oatmeal cookie; egg salad, milk, apple slices; egg salad, lemonade, apple slices; egg salad, apple juice, apple slices; egg salad, water, yogurt; egg salad, milk, yogurt; egg salad, lemonade, yogurt; egg salad, apple juice, yogurt; egg salad, water, yogurt; egg salad, milk, granola bar; egg salad, lemonade, granola bar; egg salad, apple juice, granola bar; egg salad, water, granola bar; PB&J, milk, oatmeal cookie;

Answer Key

PB&J, lemonade, oatmeal cookie; PB&J, apple juice, oatmeal cookie; PB&J, water, oatmeal cookie; PB&J, milk, apple slices; PB&J, lemonade, apple slices; PB&J, apple juice, apple slices; PB&J, water, yogurt; PB&J, milk, yogurt; PB&J lemonade, yogurt; PB&J, apple juice, yogurt; PB&J, water, yogurt; PB&J, milk, granola bar; PB&J, lemonade, granola bar; PB&J, apple juice, granola bar; PB&J, water, granola bar; Try This!: answers will vary.

Page 273

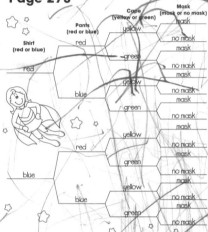

Try This!: A. Answers will vary.
B:

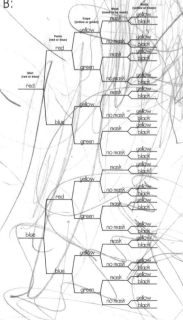

Page 274

Possible Numbers: 731, 713, 371, 317, 137, 173; 1. 6; 2. 731; 3. 137; 4. 594; Try This!: A. 479, 497, 974, 947, 749, 794; B. Answers will vary.

Page 275

4,689; 4,698; 4,869; 4,896; 4,986; 4,968; 6,489; 6,498; 6,894; 6,849; 6,948; 6,984; 8,469; 8,496; 8,964; 8,946; 8,649; 8,694; 9,846; 9,864; 9,684; 9,648; 9,486; 9,468; 1. 9,864; 2. 4,689; 3. 4,986; 4. 4,698; Try This!: answers will vary.

Page 276

1. likely; 2. likely; 3. unlikely; 4. unlikely; 5. likely; 6. Answers will vary. 7. unlikely; 8. likely; Try This!: answers will vary.

Page 277

1. 1 out of 14; 2. 2 out of 14; 3. 5 out of 14; 4. 9 out of 14; 5. 4 out of 13; 6. 2 out of 13; 7. 7 out of 13; 8. 6 out of 13; Try This!: answers will vary.

Page 278

1. 6/12; 2. 4/12; 3. 2/12; 4. stickers; 5. a car. Try This!: A. Answers will vary. B. 1:2; 1:3, 1:6

Page 279

1: Lin, Shelby, Quan; Lin, Quan, Shelby; Shelby, Quan, Lin; Shelby, Lin, Quan; Quan, Lin, Shelby; Quan, Shelby, Lin. 2: two ways (Paul, Shelby, Lin, Quan; Paul, Shelby, Quan, Lin); 3: Lin, Quan, Shelby; 4: six ways (Lin, Shelby, Quan, Paul; Lin, Shelby, Paul, Quan; Lin, Quan, Paul, Shelby; Lin, Quan, Shelby, Paul; Lin, Paul, Quan, Shelby; Lin, Paul, Shelby, Quan); Try This!: answers will vary.

Page 280

Possible outfits: striped shirt and jeans, striped shirt and cargo pants, striped shirt and shorts, dress shirt and jeans, dress shirt and cargo pants, dress shirt and shorts, sweater and jeans, sweater and cargo pants, sweater and shorts; Try This!: answers will vary.

Page 281

1: 20 pieces of gum; 2: 6 buzzers in each box; 3: 8 goofy glasses; 4: 13 packages of fake teeth; Try This!: answers will vary.

Page 282

1. 390 feet; 2. 36 feet; 3. 105 feet; 94 feet; Try This!: answers will vary.

Page 283

1. 60 cookies; 2. 120 cookies; 3. 40 boxes of cookies; 4. yes; Try This!: answers will vary.

Page 284

1. Anton carried the banana, Greg carried the apple, Fiona carried the orange, and Brady carried the grape. 2. Kit brought salad, Liza brought tamales, Luke brought chicken, and Jimmy brought pizza. Try This!: answers will vary.

Page 285

1: pages 54 and 55; 2: pages 805 and 806; 3: pages 298 and 299; 4: pages 914 and 915; Try This!: answers will vary.

Page 286

1: 291 and 453; 2: 1,210 and 1,154; 3: 10, 11, and 21; 4: 709 and 710; Try This!: answers will vary.

Page 287

1. 15 tricks, the pattern is +2; 2. a square; 3. 78, the pattern is -9, +5; 4. 12 times, The pattern is -11. Try This!: answers will vary.

Page 288

1. emerald; 2. 256 pearls; 3. diamond; Try This!: answers will vary.

Page 289

1. $100.00; 2. 3:48 P.M.; 3. 30 toys; 4. $23.00; Try This!: answers will vary.

Page 290

1. 21 miles; 2. $35.00; 3. 2:40 P.M.; 4. 4 children; Try This!: answers will vary.

CD-104538 • © Carson-Dellosa